"Carey Martin has written a simple, effective, and accessible book for the education of first-time screenwriters."
—**David Carren,** *Screenwriter and Professor at the University of Texas Rio Grande Valley*

APPLIED SCREENWRITING

Putting a vision on the page for creative and commercial video is harder than it seems, but author Carey Martin explains how to bring these tools to bear in the "work for hire" environment.

While other texts focus on writing the next award winner, this can be out of reach both logistically and financially for many. Instead, readers will learn how to write what they want the eyes of the audience to see and the ears of the audience to hear, in such a way that the Producer and Director can read the creative blueprint and bring that vision to life. The text will walk readers through a focused and practical consideration of the camera, the edit, and the sound design, in addition to a straightforward application of basic story principles. By understanding writing for video as more than creating a recorded play, readers will become more effective screenwriters and, should they wish, Producers and Directors as well.

This book is ideal for students of screenwriting and those writing scripts for message-driven video for corporate, nonprofit, and commercial production.

Carey Martin is Professor of Digital Media at Liberty University, USA. He has worked and written for local broadcast television, nonprofit educational media, Fortune 500 corporate video, and independent film before and during his academic career. He has earned multiple peer-reviewed awards for his screenwriting and directing, including for his short film *Ohfer* (2016).

APPLIED SCREENWRITING

How to Write True Scripts
for Creative and Commercial Video

Carey Martin

LONDON AND NEW YORK

Designed cover image: © Illia Uriadnikov / Alamy

First published 2024
by Routledge
4 Park Square, Milton Park, Abingdon, Oxon OX14 4RN

and by Routledge
605 Third Avenue, New York, NY 10158

Routledge is an imprint of the Taylor & Francis Group, an informa business

© 2024 Carey Martin

The right of Carey Martin to be identified as author of this work has been asserted in accordance with sections 77 and 78 of the Copyright, Designs and Patents Act 1988.

All rights reserved. No part of this book may be reprinted or reproduced or utilised in any form or by any electronic, mechanical, or other means, now known or hereafter invented, including photocopying and recording, or in any information storage or retrieval system, without permission in writing from the publishers.

Trademark notice: Product or corporate names may be trademarks or registered trademarks, and are used only for identification and explanation without intent to infringe.

British Library Cataloguing-in-Publication Data
A catalogue record for this book is available from the British Library

Library of Congress Cataloging-in-Publication Data
Names: Martin, Carey (Professor of digital media), author.
Title: Applied screenwriting : how to write true scripts for creative & commercial video / Carey Martin.
Description: Abingdon, Oxon ; New York, NY : Routledge, 2024. | Includes bibliographical references and index.
Identifiers: LCCN 2023044646 (print) | LCCN 2023044647 (ebook) | ISBN 9781032531069 (hardback) | ISBN 9781032531052 (paperback) | ISBN 9781003410317 (ebook)
Subjects: LCSH: Motion picture authorship.
Classification: LCC PN1996 .M4416 2024 (print) | LCC PN1996 (ebook) | DDC 808.06/6791—dc23/eng/20231018
LC record available at https://lccn.loc.gov/2023044646
LC ebook record available at https://lccn.loc.gov/2023044647

ISBN: 9781032531069 (hbk)
ISBN: 9781032531052 (pbk)
ISBN: 9781003410317 (ebk)

DOI: 10.4324/9781003410317

Typeset in Sabon
by Apex CoVantage, LLC

This book is dedicated to the two professional communicators who shaped my life and my career: my father, Dr. Fred L. Martin, and my mentor, Dr. Stuart Kaminsky.

CONTENTS

Acknowledgments   *xi*

1   "Applied" versus "Basic" Screenwriting   1

2   The Story: The Pulse of the Script   10

3   The Production Team: The Target for the Script   28

4   The Format: The Structure of the Script   47

5   The Scene Description: Opening the Eyes of the Audience   59

6   Camera and Lighting: Focusing the Eyes of the Audience   69

7   Editing: Moving the Eyes of the Audience   100

8   Audio: The Ears of the Audience   107

9   The Conclusion: The Effect on the Audience   116

Appendix 1: How to Format a Script . . . in the Form of a Script   *120*

*Appendix 2: The Narrative, the Split-Column, and the
North Star* 129
Appendix 3: Watching to Listen – A Filmography of Dialogue 153
Bibliography 155
Index 156

ACKNOWLEDGMENTS

Katie Thomas, my friend, colleague, screenwriting partner, and draft reviewer, is first and foremost on the acknowledgment list. Her timely and precise insights and her constant encouragement were the crucial factors in the completion of this volume. Any errors, omissions, or other imperfections are entirely my own, of course.

Hunter Richards and Rebecca Christian were the photographers for all of the illustrations for this text. Their talents, hard work, and upbeat attitudes produced everything I asked for and made the process fun besides. The three models for those photos, Sadie Sudbrock, Brian Friberg, and Desiree Baughman, were equally amazing throughout the photo shoot.

Special thanks to Jonas Larson for his permission to use the behind-the-scenes stills from his film, *Reflections*; to Hunter Richards and Rebecca Christian, again, who were also the photographers for that shoot; and to the cast and crew who consented to the use of their appearances therein: Brandon Burket, Sarah Bussard, Jonas Larson, Hunter Richards, and Caleb Smith.

Very special thanks to very special friend, Terry Perkins, for permission to use his collection for the Armorer Illustration.

Dr. Louise Benjamin, Dr. Ed Fink, Prof. Mary Beth O'Connor, and Dr. Pete Orlik added to their honors as lifetime friends and Broadcast Education Association colleagues by reviewing the proposal that became this volume. Thank you for your service at the beginning and for the cheerleading along the way.

Thanks to the editorial team at Routledge/Taylor & Francis, Rachel Feehan and Andrew Peart, and extra special thanks to Claire Margerison for getting the ball rolling.

Finally, my wife, Traci Martin, patiently gave up most of a summer to the completion of this volume. To say that this was only the tip of the iceberg of her love and support seriously understates the case.

1
"APPLIED" VERSUS "BASIC" SCREENWRITING

Greetings, Fellow Mermaids and Mermen: Today We Are Learning to Create Water

"Explaining water to a fish." We've all heard it. It's been used, reused, expanded into anecdotes, and compressed into the question "Do fish know they're wet?" When I talk with my students about the world of video (which, in this chapter, is used as the short term for all forms of recorded moving images with synchronized soundtracks, regardless of means of production or distribution), I often think of this well-worn expression.

And yet, I must remind myself – we are not fish. We are mer-people. And we made our own ocean.

It's certainly true that the audience for which you and I are writing, and we ourselves, are swimming in the ocean of video. And, from our perspective, we always have been. Consider the following. High school students in the United States, and their United Kingdom counterparts in primary school, have never seen analog television. The acronyms for the former broadcast television standards in the US and UK respectively, NTSC and PAL (never mind Russia and France's SECAM) mean nothing to them. Their parents, if they do remember the old competing standards, cannot recall a time when television was monochrome ("black and white"). Only the seasoned citizens among us can remember the time before television, when one had to go to a theater to see moving pictures; fewer still even remember when color movies were the exception and not the rule. As for silent movies . . . well, not only would one have to be truly venerable, one would need a phenomenal memory; as of this publication, Warner Brothers' release of *The Jazz Singer* is approaching its centenary.

DOI: 10.4324/9781003410317-1

As that quick history also illustrates, we are fish swimming in high-definition, full-color, multi-channel audio, "water." Also, like water, video is available virtually everywhere, 24 hours a day, 365 days a year, to almost anyone of almost every economic level. This availability exceeds relatively recent science fiction. Yesterday's starship captains had a communicator in one hand and a computer on one hip when they left their craft. Today, most of the world's adults have both combined in their smartphones, and their home TV screens are bigger than the huge main monitors on that starship bridge. Set your phone aside – does that very thought inspire a chill? – and turn off your 50+-inch home theater. You can still find HDTV on your laptop or tablet, or your highway billboards, or the end-cap display in your local superstore, or – well, where can you not see moving images?

Of course, no one living remembers the time before pictures moved. In fact, no one remembers the time before the movies had become an industry. As of this writing, the oldest person alive is 116 years old, born in 1907. Astonishing as this is, by then nickelodeons – the theaters, not the cable television network – were already flourishing. Nevertheless, there was such a time, a time when all photographs, all pictures, were stills. Consider that for a moment. Before 1890 at the earliest, no one had ever seen true moving pictures.

The historical record is vague and sometimes contradictory as to who really invented moving pictures. The turn of the 20th century was a time of technological earthquakes, but that seems to have caused shaky record-keeping. Still, it shows that the shock of those first moving pictures, once the Lumieres began projecting their efforts to group audiences, was like a glass of ice water in the face. And then, customers gulped down their films like ice water on a hot summer day. Movies like "Workers Leaving the Factory" and "Train Arriving at the Station" played to sold-out houses, not only in the Lumieres' home base of Paris, but, during their world tour, in Brussels, Bombay, London, Montreal, New York City, and Buenos Aires. The titles, incidentally, were total truth in advertising; workers left, trains arrived, and the show was over. And if the show had stopped there, moving images might have stopped too.

Fortunately, in their very first screening, the Lumieres had included a piece originally called *Le Jardinier*, "The Gardener," but much more famously known today as *L'Arroseur Arrosé*, "The Sprinkler Sprinkled." The onscreen action was unlike anything either the Lumieres or anyone else had shot to date. A man is watering a garden. Behind him, a mischievous lad steps on the hose. The man looks in the hose; the boy lifts his foot; and the man gets a face-full of water. The man whirls, catches the lad, and administers a quick punishment. With just under a minute of screen time, the Lumieres stumbled on the secret that would transform moving images from a glass of ice water into a gushing fountain, if not a firehose. The moving picture *told a story*. That simple concept was what really changed the world.

Ironically, the Lumieres themselves never truly grasped the significance of story. It was left to other early pioneers to develop. Alice Guy Blaché's *The Cabbage Fairy*, Georges Méliès' *A Trip to the Moon*, Edwin Porter's *Life of an American Fireman* and *The Great Train Robbery* were just some of the monuments of the short film storytelling that led, eventually, to features. Shortly thereafter, radio blossomed into its golden age, and the storytelling of sound-only dramas and comedies were the predecessors of the television series of today.

So, in both place and time, video surrounds us as completely as fish are surrounded by water. Unlike the fish, which didn't make their own ocean (lake, river, etc.), we did. At least, some of us "fish" have been and are still working very hard to make the media ocean. Those in front of the camera have been public figures since the moving image deluge began, or at least since Carl Laemmle turned Florence Lawrence into "the first movie star" in 1909. With the vast entertainment journalism of today, even the most casual media consumer is at least aware of the legions of people behind the scenes who make the magic happen. A few of those legions, mostly Directors, have even become celebrities in their own right. This popular "auteurist" focus, though, misses two vital points.

First, every person who works on any production is vital to the completion of the project. This is true regardless of production size or budget, from the $300 million fantastic blockbuster feature to the humblest commercial for local TV. There are no unimportant positions on a set or in a studio; unimportant positions are unhired. Each position is also crucial to production success. Even granting a Director's creative vision, how the members of the production team do their jobs creates the final audience experience. The whole really is greater than the sum of the parts.

Second, while all those parts are important for the completion of the project, one is essential even for the beginning. Novelist, short story writer, and teleplay scripter Harlan Ellison, writing in his less-famous role of motion picture critic, quoted no less an auteur than Francis Ford Coppola:

> I like to think of myself as a writer who directs. When people go to see a movie, 80 percent of the effect it has on them was preconceived and precalculated by the writer. He's the one who imagines opening with a shot of a man walking up the stairs and cutting to another man walking down the stairs. A good script has pre-imagined exactly what the movie is going to do on a story level, on an emotional level, on all these various levels. To me, that's the primary act of creation.
>
> *(Ellison 299)*

In other words, Coppola confirms both the art and the craft of writing scripts as the foundation of moving image success. This also leads us to the definition of screenwriting that will guide this book.

Screenwriting is

- the art and craft of writing story-scripts
- to create moving image media
- for contemporary audiences

Storytelling in any form is one of the oldest, if not the very oldest, of the arts. In the arts, there are not many hard-and-fast rules. The pure story can be expressed with great flexibility, with few axioms that must be followed inflexibly. Consider some of the experiments that have been carried out in novels and short stories in the last century or so. Therefore, when we apply ourselves to the first flights of imagination, we may follow our muses as they lead us. On the other hand, as some of those experiments also demonstrate, pure stream-of-consciousness may have great meaning to ourselves and possibly a limited audience but not to a mass viewership. It seems that even the muses obey some flight plans.

Crafts, in contrast, creative as they are, are bound by multiple rules. For example, carpenters' rulers and plumb lines exist for a reason. Creativity that expresses a message or accomplishes a purpose needs some standards to do so. Just so, telling video stories requires following rules in both script and production. Those rules often require an understanding of terminology; if you don't know what the terms "shot" and "cutting" mean in context, you won't grasp the meaning behind Coppola's quotation. More important, regardless of your base writing talent, if you don't understand how screenwriters communicate their ideas of shots and cuts, you will be a less effective communicator in video.

To sum up, if you are reading this book, you have an interest in writing. Specifically, you want to write scripts for video. That video will be sent out to an audience that is video saturated – in fact, super-saturated. Thus, to even be noticed by that audience, you must have more than a talent for storytelling. You must have a craftsman's understanding of all the storytelling tools used in video. This does not mean that you necessarily need to know how to *do* a shot, a cut, or any other technique. It does mean that you need to know how to *write* them.

And that is the focus of this book. A focus I call "Applied Screenwriting."

Are You Frankenstein, or Reinstein?

What, you are doubtless asking, distinguishes "Applied Screenwriting" from any other screenwriting? And what do these two notable, though fictional, scientists have to do with it?

Well, I am something of a science-fiction buff. Good science fiction is based on, or illustrates, real scientific concepts. In this case, our two example scientists illustrate the difference between basic research and applied research.

Dr. Victor Frankenstein, in Mary Shelley's classic, is a prototypical basic researcher. No one was funding his inquiry into what used to be called "things man was not meant to know." Quite the opposite in fact – virtually everyone in his fictional world was actively opposed to his research. His obsessive quest to use lightning to bring life to a humanoid creature of sewn-together body parts was entirely for his own knowledge. Of course, he imagined that this would also bring him fame and fortune, but no one had promised him that (for good reason).

On the other hand, Professor Reinstein, as he was known in the original origin story of America's super-soldier (in the Marvel Cinematic Universe retelling, he is Dr. Erskine), worked directly for the United States government. He was experimenting to turn an ordinary man into the perfect officer and gentleman. This research goal had a defined and practical purpose: the Allies defeating the Axis in World War II. Granted, he should have kept more complete notes, but perhaps it is as well he did not. This is applied research, and very applied at that.

Similarly, what I call "basic" screenwriting is driven by the writer's personal interests and imagination, its goal to expand the creativity of our field. The purest form of this is the spec script – the feature screenplay or series teleplay that one writes to demonstrate that one can in fact write. As one wit put it, a spec scriptwriter speculates that someone will want the finished script. Even feature and series scripts that are bought and paid for, though, have the common foundation that they are written primarily to entertain. They certainly have "messages," but the writer starts with the story. At least, the good ones do.

Professional writing at this level is the subject of a host of excellent texts, many of which are available from this publisher. These books, however, confirm that this kind of screenwriting is "basic" in another sense as well. The texts focus on character, setting, and plot, and how exactly the rhythms and pacing of your story need to fit the demands of cinematic features or television programs. The unstated – or in some cases stated – assumption is that your script will be handed off to a creative team. Each of these professionals will use their specialized expertise to turn your script into a completed show. In other words, many of the tools of video are left completely out of the hands of the writer.

That is correct – for that kind of screenwriting. From the $200-million-plus blockbusters of summer down to the unpublicized movies of the "dump months" of late January and February, screenwriters for studio features count themselves fortunate to be invited onto the set. In series television, where staff writers have considerably more input, the production team still has ultimate control over the production tools. One of the faster tickets out of Hollywood – or the BBC for that matter – for a series writer is presuming to offer their opinion on how a scene should be lit, shot, or cut.

The fantastic thing about our era, though, is that the outlet for video has expanded far beyond "Hollywood." For the cost of a smartphone and its

6 "Applied" versus "Basic" Screenwriting

network, aspiring filmmakers can broadcast to the world via a host of online services. Of course, these creators are unlikely to have the highly trained and experienced crews of the series and features of Tinseltown, Bollywood, or any production center in between, either. They are far more likely to perform most, if not all, of the production roles themselves.

That said, these video creators will be well served not only to understand the tools of production before they sit down to write but to apply those tools to the page from the first draft of the script. This is the first and most important aspect of what I call *Applied Screenwriting*. *Applied Screenwriting* is the process of imagining, then specifying on the page, the final results that you want the audience to see and hear. In other words, you are not simply crafting character, setting, and plot; you are writing, from draft one, how you want the script to be produced.

I contend that thinking like an Applied Screenwriter will help any screenwriter, including the student sitting down at the keyboard for their very first homework script. Still, the second and only slightly less important part of Applied Screenwriting makes the full application of these ideas not only possible but profitable. Patriot though he was, Dr. Reinstein got paid for his applied research. Just so, Applied Screenwriting in this sense, screenwriting that other people pay for, has also expanded far beyond the international production centers. Clients in every imaginable industry are paying for videos that professionally and creatively communicate their messages. The key words here, of course, are professional and creative.

Communication researcher Dr. Harold Lasswell proposed a model for communication that I think works well as a framework for the professional side of that equation:

- *Who?*
- *Says What?*
- *In Which Channel?*
- *To Whom?*
- *With What Effect?*

(117)

Who is the Sender – the person who starts the communication. If you're a spec writer, that "Who" is you. If you're an Applied Screenwriter, it's the client – who may also be you, if you are sending your own message. Regardless, the "who" shapes all that proceeds from it. You need look no further than the "influencers" of social media for this. While throngs of would-be celebrities address the same subject, each puts their own personal stamp on their videos (or tries to).

Says What is the Message itself. Again, in a purely entertainment script, that's the story. In Applied Screenwriting, it is the story plus the conscious message that is meant to be conveyed through story.

This needs some unpacking. I contend that all stories in every medium communicate a message. This is because, as we will discuss in a later chapter, all stories have a Protagonist – a hero. The author wants us to cheer for the hero. It follows that the hero will only do things that the author believes their audience can cheer, or at least that the author wants the audience to cheer. Those "cheer-able" actions illustrate the message, the theme, or what some call the "North Star" of the story – the point toward which the entire story points.

In a "basic" script, I also contend this North Star should arise organically. The Lumieres left no indication that they made "Sprinkler Sprinkled" to communicate any profound theme. Still, the fact that the little prankster is caught and punished clearly conveys "Crime doesn't pay" – or, less seriously, "Don't be a brat." If the North Star message you set out with is not exactly what you have when the story is complete – well, a complete discussion of how and why that happens will be a book itself. Still, as long as the North Star that you find in the process of creation is the one that the audience finds in the act of observation, you may consider your work a success.

On the other hand, one of the primary challenges of most Applied Screenwriting is that the message comes first. You may very well have to adjust your story to communicate "Buy insurance," or "Here's how to write a professional email," or "Trust me, I'm a reliable influencer." If you understand that message is your North Star from the beginning, it is easier to steer your story toward it.

In Which Channel is the Medium – in this case, video. At least, that is the premise for both basic and applied writing in this field. Another of the challenges of Applied Screenwriting is recognizing that video is not always the best medium for the message. Just as some meetings could be emails, so could some videos. Once it's determined that video is the desired medium, though, a further consideration is the final screen. Smartphone screens have advantages of portability and convenience that IMAX does not; IMAX far outstrips all other video media in visual detail and emotional impact. On the other hand, smartphones have the disadvantage of an almost universally distracted audience, while IMAX is obviously far ahead in expense of production and limitations of release. Understanding which your audience will use goes a long way toward determining the effectiveness of your video. Speaking of whom...

To Whom is, of course, the Audience – the people who watch. Even spec writers who dream of their creations being #1 at the box office (and streaming services and home video sales) focus their scripts on segments of the total feature audience. The principle applies still more in television. The major American networks (ABC, CBS, FOX, NBC, and CW) still concentrate on broadcasting, attempting to provide something for everybody, but the "everybody" they aim for changes throughout the day.

The myriad cable networks carry this targeting a step further, to "narrowcasting." ESPN, the most profitable US channel, is built for sports fans;

if you're not, they certainly won't stop you from watching, but they won't cry if you don't either. Every demographic consideration is factored into the programming decisions, including nationality. BBC One and BBC America do not carry identical lineups; ESPN and ESPN Deportes, obviously, don't even share a language.

The advent of YouTube and other open-access video streamers has ushered in a new era of "nichecasting." While a fortunate few YouTubers have millions of subscribers, there are millions more whose subscribers are measured in thousands or even hundreds. Applied Screenwriting can take this even a step further, to a script tailored to an audience of dozens – what might be termed "lasercasting." Fortunately, such small audiences can usually be described quite precisely because a client has commissioned said video for the audience of their employees. The point is, the more specific the audience, the more tailored your script can be to reaching them.

To What Effect is exactly what it says on the label – the effect. The basic screenwriter seeks to entertain, in the sense of engaging the emotions of their audience. The Applied Screenwriter seeks to consciously inform, or persuade, or even instruct – but the Applied Screenwriter must also entertain if they hope to convey that message. In other words, the Applied Screenwriter crafts emotionally engaging messages to specific purposes – sometimes her or his own, but often those of a second party.

Further, especially in today's digital era, the question of interactivity often arises. Writing apps, video games, and the like are beyond the scope of this text. However, I once heard transmedia Producer Stephen Dinehart put it succinctly: "Interactivity is a good conversation." Even if you are doing a one-shot, client-commissioned instructional video, your goal should be to start a conversation among your audience about the application of your message. If you are reaching out to wider audiences via social media, you not only hope for an initial conversation, you aim for an ongoing relationship, a back-and-forth between you and your audience. Your Applied Script, thus, should be the beginning of a process of mediated conversation leading to a mediated relationship with your audience.

This brings us back around to the creative side of the question. Your audience, even if – especially if – they are required by a boss or teacher to watch the video, is comparing what they see and hear to what they see and hear every day on their entertainment screens. Those screens engage audience emotions because they show stories, and those stories initiate the conversations and self-conversations of the viewers. To effectively communicate your message, you need to tell entertaining stories in your Applied Scripts as well; and, at the risk of repetition, you need to imagine all the tools of video at work to tell them.

The subsequent chapters of this book are written to guide just such imagination. Chapter 1, as you have read, introduces the fundamental concept of

Applied Screenwriting. Chapter 2 outlines the underlying fundamental of all scripts, the Story. Chapter 3 describes the differing roles of the true readers of your script, the Production Team. Chapter 4 explicates the primary Formats of scripts and the importance of those structures. Chapter 5 explains the Scene Description and writing it as exactly what the audience sees. Chapter 6 unpacks the functions of the Camera and the Lighting and writing them as how the audience sees, and Chapter 7 explains Editing and writing it as the order of what the audience sees. Chapter 8 brings in the concepts of Audio, writing for what the audience hears. Chapter 9 brings all together in a discussion of the effect on the audience, and the Appendices look at specific examples of scripting.

In each chapter, there will be a Primary Question that focuses the heart of said chapter. That includes the following one.

The First Primary Question

Whether you are writing for your local volunteer group's social media video, or for the next half-billion-dollar conglomerate multiplex blockbuster, I urge you to keep in mind these words of wisdom I received at the beginning of my career. Dr. Fred Martin, one of the wisest communicators I ever knew (and my dad), stated this Primary Question in two parts: "In any job, know who the boss is, and what the boss wants." If you are commissioned by a client, you must understand who they are and what they want, and then make that the "North Star" of your script. If you are Applied Scriptwriting for yourself, you must view yourself in the same light: if I were paying someone else to make this video for me, what image do I want them to convey of me, and what message do I want with that image? The more clearly you understand this from the beginning, the better your story will be from the start. Thus, the story is the subject of our next chapter.

Works Cited

Ellison, Harlan. *Harlan Ellison's Watching*. Underwood-Miller, 1989.

Lasswell, Harold. "The Structure and Function of Communication in Society." *The Communication of Ideas*. Edited by Lyman Bryson, Harper & Row, 1948, pp. 37–51.

2
THE STORY

The Pulse of the Script

The Normal Pulse, or, "It's Alive! IT'S ALIVE!"

As already acknowledged, there are literally thousands of books on screenwriting and scriptwriting. There are even more thousands of books on storywriting in general and media-making as a field. I own quite a few of them, and I've read quite a few more. At the end of this book, I'll even recommend some for further reading. None of them have the precise focus of this book, which is why I undertook the writing in the first place.

I will, though, hammer home the three essential points I have gained from all of them.

- All good stories have a structure, like all living people have a pulse.
- That structure is as regular as a human pulse.
- Without that structure, your story is in the same shape as a person without a pulse.

"That's nice," you may be thinking, "but, if this were a medical book, you'd show us what normal human pulse looks like on an electrocardiogram. So . . . what's the 'pulse' of a story look like?"

That's a valid and straightforward question. The answer is equally straightforward:

All stories are about individual people, and all stories have a beginning, a middle, and an end.

Simple, right? At this point I can say, "Go thou and do likewise," and you're ready to rock and roll. Except – simple is not easy, or obvious. Walking to the

North Pole is simple, after all: just walk north until every direction is south, and you're there. Unfortunately, there are more than a few complications along the way. Further, you're not going to know which way is north without a compass. So, let's unpack that statement a bit, by applying it to the simplest of stories.

> Jack and Jill
> Went up a hill
> To fetch a pail of water
> Jack fell down
> And broke his crown
> And Jill came tumbling after.

Fortunately, for Jill, she'd recorded Jack's fall on her smartphone first. She then posted it to social media, where it went viral, and eventually got Jill (and Jack, once he recovered) their own reality TV series.

You've probably heard this before, and from a very young age – minus my own modern addition, of course. You probably never thought before that this and all nursery rhymes are very, very short examples of the story pulse.

All stories are about individual people...

In this case, a person named Jack and another person named Jill. Given the time and place of origin – the United Kingdom in the mid-1700s – we can guess that Jack is male (the text confirms this later) and Jill is female, though of course today that need not be the case. Beyond that, what do we know about Jill and Jack?

Nothing. Except the only two facts that are essential: Jack and Jill are people, and each is an individual. The nursery rhyme doesn't say "A couple went up a hill." It doesn't even say "Two humans went up a hill." It gives them names. Names are the signifiers of individuality and personhood, even in a nursery rhyme. Thus, even the simplest of stories is about individual people.

I can't stress this enough. Some of my favorite individual people in stories include

- a blue-and-purple furred working-class monster
- an ambulatory tree who communicates eloquently with just three (well, a fourth in one memorable line) words
- an innocent baby with an insatiable appetite, huge ears, and green skin
- a rabbit with a quick wit and a Brooklyn accent
- a happy-go-lucky cucumber with a goofy grin

The importance of names notwithstanding, I doubt I need to name or picture those characters. (And I won't, copyright and trademark permissions costing what they do.) You are probably recalling your own favorites from the world of animation. The scholarly term of anthropomorphism, the attribution of human personality or characteristics to something nonhuman, does not quite cover what happens in these stories. What the creators of all these characters did was take it a step further: "What if we took whole human personalities and put them inside animals, vegetables, monsters, cars, fish, or whatever? Wouldn't they *really be people*?" Joyously, these creative artists were correct. The covering doesn't matter; the personality is the personhood.

Of course, these people might have some abilities that you and I lack. The alien baby might be able to move things with his mind. The tree might be able to regrow itself from a single twig. The rabbit might be able to burrow around the world in a matter of minutes (if only he could ever make the correct turn at Albuquerque). They are still people. The individual is more important than the ability – a key point to keep in mind if you want to write fantasy, science-fiction, or superhero scripts. Just listen to fans of those genres talk. They talk about Harry and Ron and Hermione, or Luke and Han and Leia, or Tony and Steve and Natasha. They talk, in short, about people.

We could spend a lot of time and pages describing these people, as in fact their creators did. We could do the same for Jack and Jill, making note of their physical characteristics, emotional life, intellectual makeup, quirks, tastes, and so forth. In the video realm, that level of detail is only necessary and possible in long-form entertainments – feature-length movies or series television. Nonetheless, it is possible to create believable characters even within the context of a television commercial. Insurance commercials have provided plentiful examples of this in recent years. One company's team of white-coated heroes includes a preternaturally cheerful and product-obsessed leader, her goofy sidekick with an impressive array of breathtaking talents, and a snarky but effective "third banana." Another attracts customers with a bumbling parody-cop and his flightless bird partner. A third turns the eccentricity approach on its head, showing the bemused interactions of an "average guy" agent with a roster of famous pro athletes who display ever more offbeat behavior.

Whether for long-form features and series, brief tales like nursery rhymes, and short scripts such as the primary subjects of this book, we need only ask one basic question about our people, and then determine two fundamental things about them, to turn them into Characters.

The Basic Question: Protagonist or Antagonist?

The essential question about every Character is, "Are they a protagonist, or an antagonist?" Tomes have been written about those two terms. For our purposes, it's simple: do you want your audience to cheer *for* that person or *against* them?

That's it. If, watching your finished project, the audience cheers when a character succeeds, they're a Protagonist; if they cheer when they don't, an Antagonist.

"Fair enough," you are probably thinking, "but how do I make sure my viewers cheer for and against the people I want them to cheer for and against?" Again, we're at a point where simplicity does not equal ease. However, we're also at a point where simplicity points toward further simplicity. In my experience:

> Both memorable Protagonists and memorable Antagonists are mixtures of virtue and vice; the difference is which does each embrace.

Growing up, one of my favorite novels was Mark Twain's *The Adventures of Huckleberry Finn*. Even then, much of the language, though time-and-place accurate, grated on my ears. In the 21st century, I understand and respect that many people simply cannot bear certain words. If you can, though, I ask you to think for a moment about Huck. In the novel, Huck smokes like the proverbial chimney at an age when his worst habit should be bubble gum. He regards almost all the manners and mores of "society" – even the humble society in which he lives – as a house of horrors. Worst of all, Huck is a self-confessed casual thief and almost incessant liar.

On the other hand, Huck also repeatedly shows himself to be clever and resourceful, for example in faking his own death to escape his abusive father. He also shows himself to be oddly humble, in that very episode comparing how he did it to how his best friend Tom Sawyer would have and thinking Tom would've done better. Most important, Huck consistently shows himself overflowing with the vital human virtue of empathy. In his brief and tragic friendship with Buck Grangerford, in his longer and equally poignant relationship with Mary Jane Wilks, even in his dealings with the deplorable "Duke" and "King," when the chips are down Huck's heart goes out to others and especially to the underdog. Ultimately, this is demonstrated with Jim, where Huck's empathy moves him to an act of almost incalculable courage.

Now consider the world's most famous vampire, Count Dracula. Set aside the relationship to the historical figure Vlad the Impaler (no angel himself). The very idea of a mysterious, titled, wealthy aristocrat, with all the privilege that that implies, who preys on innocent young women under the cover of night is both horrifying and too close to some modern headlines. Add that this paragon of "the elite" is "undead," unageing, with a cornucopia of supernatural abilities, and can only be destroyed by a specific and very limited set of attacks, and you have the stuff of literal nightmares.

And yet . . . and yet . . . the Count is undeniably charismatic, even without using magic or psychic powers. His charm is matched by his unfailing courtesy, except when he's interrupted while sucking someone's blood. (After all, who among us really enjoys being interrupted at a meal?) He is both highly intelligent and very well learned, not necessarily the same thing. He is also a man of impeccable if dated taste. Finally, even in his very first literary account, there is a hint of sadness in his demeanor; the undead may live forever, but only by never seeing the sun. Small wonder that the Count has been portrayed as the outright hero in some media. Even as the villain, his blend of vice and virtue makes Dracula a fascinating antagonist because Dracula is a fascinating person.

Working in short-form video does not change this principle. Whether you personally prefer Flo or Jamie or Doug or Jake, you can easily recognize their strengths and weaknesses. Using the anthropomorphism approach, one company has personified "Mayhem" to create an antiheroic Protagonist. His infuriating ability to appear in an endless stream of guises is offset by his obvious glee in wreaking havoc on the unfortunate holders of cut-rate insurance policies.

This brings up an important point; if you choose an antihero protagonist, you must work doubly hard to ensure your protagonist is likable. Likability is a key component of persuasion, which is a primary goal of Applied Screenwriting. In his best-selling text, *Influence: the Psychology of Persuasion*, Dr. Robert Cialdini enumerated the following factors to create liking:

- Physical attractiveness of persuader (171)
- Similarity of persuader to audience (173)
- Compliments from persuader to audience (174)
- Contact or familiarity of persuader to audience (176–77), as long as it is accompanied by cooperation between persuader and audience (181–82)
- Association between persuader and conditions desirable to audience (188), even if that association is produced through deliberate conditioning

(193)

These factors present different levels of challenge for the screenwriter. We can specify that our Protagonist is both physically attractive and within our Audience's demographics. As examples such as Loki in the MCU demonstrate, the personal charisma of the actor goes a long way as well – especially in connecting the audience to an antiheroic Protagonist. Unless we are doing the casting ourselves, though, we must trust the Director and the Producer to accomplish the feat of finding the perfect actor. On the other hand, we can write dialogue that our Audience finds agreeable or even flattering. As the example of Mayhem suggests, humor goes a long way toward making a character likeable. Still, give your audience a person with name, vice, and virtue in thirty seconds or less, and you create character; add one or more of these likability factors, and that character becomes highly persuasive.

These factors can also be reinforced at the script stage with descriptions that provide culturally appropriate visual clues to which of our Characters are Protagonists and Antagonists. For example, in Western culture, light clothing and bright illumination are associated with positive characters. Dark costumes and shadowy lighting connote more negative ones, at least traditionally – Batman and Chuck "Good Guys Wear Black" Norris notwithstanding. We will discuss visual description in much more detail shortly. For now, take comfort that your audience readily draws on its years of viewing to rapidly pick up such clues about the nature of your Characters.

Speaking of which, let's get back to the two Characters we started discussing. Jack and Jill, after all, are still waiting to begin their epic adventure. The unknown originator of the rhyme, popularly known as "Mother Goose," has given us the foundation to build on; to turn the nursery rhyme into a five-minute online video or a multi-installment feature franchise, give J & J a meaningful virtue, a significant vice, and a choice to make between the two . . . and then send them up the hill.

All stories have a beginning, a middle, and an end. . .

And . . . so what? Everything in the physical universe has a beginning, middle, and end. As humorist P.J. O'Rourke observed, though, reality usually lacks plot and organization (233). That's the thing that sets good stories apart from everything else – an organized plot. In fact, most of the other screenwriting books on the market spend hundreds of pages on organizing your plot. This is mostly because those books deal with theatrical features or television series. The different demands of movies and TV lead to different and more detailed approaches to breaking down the plot. Nevertheless, virtually everyone acknowledges the primary organization of plot in English-language media: the three-act structure.

The Beginning: Act I – The Setup

As Rogers and Hammerstein famously noted, the beginning is a very good place to start. Of course, this implies that you have a very good beginning. So, what makes a good beginning, a good Act I? Once again, simple-not-easy; just set up the entire rest of your story. That setup answers three basic questions:

1. Who are the Protagonists?
2. What is the Setting?
3. What starts the Conflict?

Who Are the Protagonists?

In act I of your story, you introduce the audience to the people you want them to cheer for, and you give them a reason to do so. New screenwriters with experience in other creative writing may be moved to create detailed character descriptions and histories for these people, laying out their entire lives before page 1 of the script. In screenwriting these are called "backstories." Having created great backstories, we are tempted to share them in Act I. By all means, develop your characters' backstories; but at all costs, do *not* share them in Act I.

Your audience neither wants nor needs to know the complete psychosocial history of your protagonist in the first pages of your script. What they want to know is the person they should focus on; what they need to know is why they should do so. For that reason, I emphasize "*introduce*" and "*a* reason."

When you introduce one friend to another in real life, you don't give them every life detail of each other. Usually what's said is "Jack, this is Jill; Jill, Jack," and then you mention one thing they may find interesting about each other. Of course, in real life you have the advantage of personally knowing both persons you're introducing. That's why you say things like "Jill's a fellow [whatever their school mascot], Jack"; or "Jill's planning a vacation to [wherever she's going] – Jack just got back from there"; or "Jack's a big fan of [whoever] too, Jill." What that thing is doesn't matter much if it establishes a connection between the two of them. You also have another advantage; two people, once introduced, will generally converse with each other, thus sharing details about themselves that they want the other to know. Sometimes, these details will reveal things in common; Jill's looking forward to trying restaurants on vacation, and Jack's a big foodie too. Sometimes, differences that nevertheless can be explored; at their mutual alma mater, Jill studied nuclear physics while Jack learned Romance languages. At any rate, you can leave further discussion to the introduced persons.

Neither of these advantages applies in screenwriting. You're introducing characters to an audience. We can predict you will not know every audience member personally – at least, we hope your audiences are big enough that you won't – and those viewers have only two responses to your character; keep watching or stop. Therefore, your introduction of the character must be more than just a name, and your connection must matter very much. In Act I, you must quickly, very quickly, show your audience the essentials of your character, and an equally essential connection with them.

By "essentials of character," I mean that the first act – we're still there, remember – of the story will not make sense unless we know this thing about that character. To follow the tale, is it essential that the audience know your protagonist's profession? Show it. To understand the plot, is it essential that they know your main character's family? Show it. To grasp the story, is it essential that they know your hero has a recurring rash in an uncomfortable area? Within the limits of your rating system and your audience's tastes, show it.

These essential qualities engage a viewer's mind with your character. The essential connection, on the other hand, engages the viewer's heart. For example, showing the protagonist unlocking and entering an office that says "Joan Doe, Private Investigator" tells your audience a key fact about who they are and what they do. But, unless you are creating your video for a private eye convention, your audience may or not be heart-connected. After all, the history of media chronicles countless detectives on big and small screens. If, however, you show Ms. Doe stopping short inside and reacting in shock to that office in shambles, obviously having been ransacked, now your audience is engaged because anyone can relate to the invasion of their personal space.

I should emphasize, even at this early stage, the essential, crucial, vital word in the previous two paragraphs: *Show*. If I have one indispensable concept to pass on, it's that idea. Show, show, show – and tell only as a last resort. I should also emphasize that the mind connection and the heart connection are not mutually exclusive; they're both/and, not either/or. In American culture particularly, the private investigator has been a heroic icon at least since the days of Dashiell Hammett and Raymond Chandler, thus giving Ms. Doe at least a chance to engage the audience without further effort. On the flip side, the outrage we all share with Ms. Doe is followed immediately by two intellectual questions: who ransacked her office, and why?

We will return to those mysteries shortly, but before we do, Ms. Doe's office provides an excellent opportunity to illustrate the second major question of Act I:

What Is the Setting?

Every story takes place in a place and a time. That is the setting. Once again, what we show the viewer must be essential to the plot. In the previous illustration, Ms. Doe's office may be on the second floor of a run-down urban tenement. It may be on the twentieth floor of a gleaming new skyscraper. It may be on the ground floor of a quiet suburban professional center. Whichever we choose, it will make a great difference to the audience's understanding of the character. It will also make a difference if, through her office window, the viewer glimpses the Empire State Building, or the Tower of Big Ben, or the Sydney Opera House.

So much is straightforward. What is less obvious is the equal importance of time, and of showing that to the audience as well. Consider New York City, or London, or Sydney, a hundred years ago (that's only the 1920s, after all); then mentally advance decade by decade to the present. This mental exercise is made easier since many historical eras of the major cities of the world have become familiar to us, thanks to more than a century of movies and three-quarters of a century of TV. Small towns and rural areas of the globe have also been onscreen, though to a lesser extent. Fortunately, once we remind ourselves of that, we realize there are virtually as many visual indicators of time as of space. For example, Ms. Doe may pull up in front of her office in a Stutz Bearcat, a Tesla, or a Spinner hover-car; the country fields around her city may be plowed with oxen, or mules, or steam tractors, or the newest diesel model. Whichever you choose, you have just told the audience the general era of the story they are going to see. Times more specific than this may also be shown without referring to clock or calendar, even in short form. In the United States, jack-o-lanterns, fireworks, and snowflakes in advertising send the message of the seasons as surely as the calendar; in the United Kingdom, Boxing Day and Guy Fawkes Night send the same message.

On the other hand, there's nothing necessarily wrong with a more on-the-nose tactic if you need it. A headline or breaking news story seen by your characters, for example, will establish a precise time for them and the audience. If set in the past, historical references work too. The classic film *Casablanca*, written by Julius and Philip Epstein and Howard Koch and directed by Michael Curtiz, contains the following exchange:

Rick (Humphrey Bogart): Sam, if it's December 1941 in Casablanca, what time is it in New York?
Sam (Dooley Wilson): Uh, my watch stopped.
Rick: I bet they're asleep in New York. I bet they're asleep all over America.

(109)

In that moment, we know that the characters are working out their destinies between December 1 and 6, 1941. And we know that every American of the time is about to get a particularly vivid answer to the third question...

What Starts the Conflict?

Rick has been involved in the conflict long before a sleeping America got its wake-up call. This is the reason we care about him before Pearl Harbor. Without conflict, there is no story. With conflict, there is. In fact, the conflicts in *Casablanca*'s seventy-two-hour time frame fill a movie as well as stories set over much longer periods. There are two reasons for this.

First, there is a mix of both external and internal conflicts: opposition to our hero from outside, and opposition to our hero from within himself. In Rick's case, his external conflict comes from the Nazis. His internal conflict in great measure stems from his personal mix of vice and virtue we've established as necessary to all memorable characters.

Second, all the conflicts – and at one time or another Rick is in greater or lesser conflict with every character except his own employees – favor the antagonist. The hero should ideally always start at a disadvantage. This is the reason that the term "David and Goliath story," though originating in Jewish and Christian scripture, is familiar worldwide to people of all faiths and no faith at all. In *Casablanca's* primary external conflict, the imbalance of power between a lone and retired freedom fighter in "Vichy French" territory and the aristocratic but thoroughly Nazi Major Strasser is obvious. Less obvious is the imbalance between Rick and his friendlier rivals. Frenemy Captain Renault is the chief of police, who can and does shut down Rick's business on a pretext; Rick cannot return the favor. His rival saloon operator, Signor Ferrari, is the respected and influential head of all illegal activities in Casablanca; Rick holds no such lofty position. Even his romantic rival, Victor Laszlo, has the not-inconsiderable advantage of already being married to the lady they both love. The imbalance in Rick's internal conflict takes the whole film to convey, but – at the risk of spoilers – the natural human desire for self-preservation, the pain of a lost love, and the hope that the love might be regained all line up on one side of the question. Only Rick's conscience and principles stand on the other side of the scales.

"Of course, that's a feature film," you are probably thinking. "And you've already said that's not the focus of this book. How does a conflict work in the world we work in?" Again, our friendly neighborhood insurers – at any rate, their ad agencies – provide useful examples. As of this writing, his would-be customers are trying to get a special "personal" rate by oversharing personal info with the stalwart Jake. Jake stands also as an example of basic internal conflict. His desire to serve his customers notwithstanding, he is clearly uncomfortable with the awkward situation they put him in. Meanwhile, Mayhem tells the viewer exactly what havoc he will unleash, and then does so hilariously. Conflict need not take long to create; as these examples show, it can even be funny.

Now let's return to Jane Doe, Private Eye. She parks her vehicle in front of her office; she unlocks and walks into her office; and she sees it has been turned upside down. Now we add an internal conflict; the searchers left a note saying only, "Let this go or your dad gets it." All four points could easily be done in thirty seconds of screen time. In those thirty seconds, we've presented our protagonist, sketched our setting, and created both external and internal conflicts – and launched the story.

That launch is better known as the inciting incident, the key to which is

Everything was as it had always been . . . AND THEN ONE DAY. . . .

Though I wish it were, that catchphrase is not original to me. I heard it at one of the many great seminars I've attended through the years, but I cannot for the life of me recall which or who said it. Still the statement itself has stayed with me to this day.

"Everything was as it had always been" – that's protagonist and setting, both of which might have remained as they had always been, unchanged more or less, even-keeled more or less, and audience interest very much less. "AND THEN ONE DAY . . ." something happened to force change, to disrupt the protagonist or the setting or both, in short to start the conflict. And when the conflict starts, the story starts.

Speaking of which, our friends from the land of nursery rhymes are ready to launch their story. "Jack and Jill went up the hill to fetch a pail of water." "Mother Goose" compressed all of Act I (and Act II, but we will get there in a moment) into one short sentence. We are introduced to our Protagonists, Mr. Jack and Ms. Jill; our Setting, the Hill; and the Conflict, a lack of water. Further, we learn something about each.

First, the Conflict is essential. Water is one of the three basic human needs, after air and before food. Further, water can be used for many things besides drinking. Perhaps Jack and Jill need to wash something, even themselves. Perhaps Jack and Jill need water as an ingredient for something else: a recipe for soup, a mixture of paint, a formula for the elixir of unending youth. Perhaps they need the water to refill the boiler on their steampunk dirigible. We are not told the specifics, but part of the genius of the poem is that even the most basic assumption is a need, not a want. The stakes, in other words, are high.

Second, the Setting is challenging. Jack and Jill must go up the hill to get their water. Water, on its own, flows downhill. That being the case, why didn't our Protagonists simply wait for the water to get to them? If the water is flowing down another side of the hill from the side where they currently stand, why not walk around the hill instead of up it? Something about the setting apparently either prevents water from obeying the law of gravity, prevents our protagonists from taking the easiest route to the water, or possibly both. Regardless, the setting seems to be part of the problem, not the solution.

Third, our Protagonists certainly possess a virtue and possibly have a vice. Jack and Jill need the water; they have none; they know where the water is; they start to climb the hill to get it. Our Jill and Jack are no slackers; a strong work ethic is their key characteristic – possibly also a sense of adventure, since we've established that the setting is part of the problem. On the other hand, it is just possible that the setting is only slowing the natural progress of the water, and it would have reached our intrepid hillclimbers eventually. Impatience may be a part of their natures as well; they simply may not have wanted to take the time to wait.

Talking of time, the question of how much time to spend on each Act often comes up at this point. Some writers recommend a formula in which a certain percentage of the screen time is reserved for each act. The most common is 25% for Act I, 50% for Act II, 25% for Act III. Those percentages, in their views, should not change much, regardless of the finished production time. In other words, a 120-minute movie gets about thirty minutes for Act I, a sixty-second commercial gets fifteen seconds.

My recommendation is: *As long as you need and as short as you can as required by the medium and the story.* If you are introducing your Protagonist and your Setting to an audience that is unfamiliar with either, you will need more screen time to create that familiarity. On the other hand, the opposite is also true. Another Humphrey Bogart classic, *The Maltese Falcon* (written and directed by John Huston), was set in then-present-day San Francisco. Its private eye protagonist, Sam Spade, was already known to the audience from Dashiell Hammett's novel and from various short stories, not to mention two previous (and much less remembered today) motion pictures. With a feature-length runtime of approximately an hour and forty minutes, the Huston/Bogart movie goes from first frame to Inciting Incident in just under ten. Our commercial stories move exponentially faster. Jake is told immediately, "I want the personal rate, and so I'll share [insert laughably awkward personal quirk]." Mayhem introduces his current persona in the first line he delivers. The same principle applies in our runtimes; as noted above, we could easily knock out the first Act of Jane Doe's adventures in half a minute. And, again, "Mother Goose" did it in a sentence for Jack and Jill.

For another perspective on building Act I, we can consult the wisdom of J. Michael Straczynski. Mr. Straczinsky has written for virtually every medium – newspapers, animation, live-action television, features, graphic novels, "regular" novels – and has won awards for most of them. In his text *The Complete Book of Screenwriting*, he created an "equation" (his term), the first half of which is *Characterization + Desire = Goal* (25). Characterization we've discussed; Desire is what that character wants; Goal is what they'll do to get what they want. This concept confirms what we've already said about the centrality of character. Lots of people might want exactly the same thing in the same situation, and in fact many do; there are a limitless number of stories because each of those identical desires is sought by a different and unique (in the true sense of that word) person.

But this is only the first half of the equation. The second half is part of the second act.

The Middle: Act II – The Follow-Through

I typed "second act hardest act to write screenplay" into my search engine and hit enter. It generated more than a hundred and fifty million results. I changed screenplay to script and drew similar numbers. Clearly, a lot of us writers know where we want our stories to start, and probably where we want them to end, but the journey from point alpha to point omega gives us challenges.

Let's go back to our rhyme. Here is Mother Goose's Act II: "Jack and Jill went up a hill." That's it. That's not much help.

Or is it?

Recall the first half of Straczinsky's equation. ***Characterization + Desire = Goal*** (25). Somebody wants something and will take some action to get it. Fair enough, but that won't necessarily generate pulse-pounding stories. As I wrote this, I realized (like our hero and heroine) that I was thirsty. I went to the refrigerator and got a drink. Those are facts, but a story they do not make. Why not? Because nothing was stopping me.

Straczinsky's equation has two halves. The second and equally important half is ***Goal + Conflict = Story*** (25). Somebody wants something and will take some action to get it; something or someone is stopping them. The Protagonist must be *stopped* in order for the story to *start*.

I can hardly emphasize this enough. As a college instructor, I have more than once received two genres of this nonstory: the Road Trip Script and the Young Love Script. In the Road Trip Script, two or more friends happily pack up and leave campus for a fun break. They go to a fun place and do fun things. They come back happy. The End. In the Young Love Script, boy meets girl (note: these are not thoughtless concessions to the patriarchy – I have yet to receive a version of this with other genders); boy and girl fall instantly, madly, and passionately in love; boy and girl go on wonderful dates; boy gives girl a ring worth as much as an economy car; boy and girl graduate on Saturday and get married on Sunday. The End. Now, it is my sincere hope for all my students, and all of you reading this, that your vacations and your romances are as trouble-free and satisfying as the Road Trip and Young Love put together. If they are, though, please don't write about them. They may look like scripts, but they're not stories. I repeat: to have a story, something must temporarily stop your protagonist.

What's stopping Jack and Jill? They're at the bottom of the hill, and the water's at the top. That may not seem much of an obstacle. Still, the course that they must take to overcome the conflict literally illustrates the key to the second act; the Protagonists move toward achieving their goal, in a pattern of Rising Action.

Rising Action means that, following the inciting incident, the Protagonist will face increasing Intensity and Complication as she moves toward her goal. Intensity refers to the energy of the actions taken to move toward the goal, and to the emotional intensity behind them. Generally, a hill gets steeper as one approaches the top; Jack and Jill will have to expend more energy the closer they get to their goal. Complication refers to the path toward the goal; in most stories, that path is anything but a straight line. Here it seems that Jack and Jill's chronicler falls short. All we are told is, needing water, they went up the hill.

The anonymous author of this tale, however, was not ignoring the principle of Rising Action. Instead, she or he was obeying a practical rule of storytelling: *There is a direct relationship between the rising action of the story and the time available to tell it.* The more time you have in which to tell your Story, the more complications you can and should bring in; conversely, less time means less complication. By definition, nursery rhymes are short. Jack and Jill do not have time to wander in the wilderness. They have got to get up that hill fast. In short, the less time you have for your story, the faster your intensity should increase.

On the flip side, more time means more gradual ramp-up of emotions and energy. If we were doing "Jack and Jill: The Motion Picture," all we now have to do is throw more and more complications at our climbers. Is the hill in fact a dormant volcano, which is showing signs of ending its dormancy? Does the Hill Weather Service show an approaching hurricane, or blizzard, or tsunami? Are there wolves on the hill? Or werewolves? This does not mean that you should start a longer form script at "low energy," incidentally. If you are writing an action film, it's fine to start with action. Just realize that whatever energy you open with, the audience expects much more by the time you hit the Crisis.

The Crisis is to the second act what the inciting incident is to the first; the gateway to the next act. The action has risen to its peak of intensity, the conflict has reached its height, and the audience is asking that crucial question: "What happens next?" Applying this to the adventure of Jane Doe, we would adjust the mystery to the time of our finished piece. If we are doing an online video, with a time window measured in seconds, there might be very little or none. "I recognize that handwriting!" Jane says, and with lightning speed, we are at the Crisis. The Antagonist has a weapon pointed at Jane's dad, and Jane's decision determines what happens next. We've got a good model for this in our nursery rhyme; it too compensates for the lack of complication by the speed with which it ramps up the intensity. "Jack fell down, and broke his crown, and. . . ." "Crown," in this case, is used as a synonym for "head." Ouch. Poor Jack. Mr. Mayhem was apparently at work here too. But notice that one little three-letter word at the end. That word is the lead into the final act.

The End: Act III – The Resolution

A peculiar point about the third act is its beginning. Some stylists argue that Act III begins not only after the Crisis but also after the Climax – the ultimate point of contention of the major conflict of the story. Others affirm that the Crisis always ends Act II, and the Climax begins Act III. As I illustrated above, I tend to agree with the Crisis-end side. However, I firmly believe that, unlike the Inciting Incident, the transition between II and III can be much smoother and less abrupt.

Jack and Jill's adventure is an illustration of this point. "Jack fell down, and broke his crown, and Jill came tumbling after." Is the crisis Jack's fall, and the climax his broken head? Or is Jack's whole mishap the crisis, and Jill's tumble the climax? Critics could probably debate this endlessly. Jack is down, badly injured; Jill has fallen also; and they never get their water.

Good as Straczynski's Equation is, years of sharing it with students prompted me to add a clarification. "Character + Desire = Goal, Goal + Conflict = Story"; Martin's Clarification is, *Story + Resolution = GOOD Story*. Whatever the Conflict is, for the Story to truly work, it must be resolved. A resolution requires two things. First, whether the Protagonist achieves her or his Goal – are they able to accomplish what they set out to do to obtain their Desire? Second and equally important, does the Protagonist obtain their Desire – do they get what they truly want or need? I emphasize the word "truly" in that sentence. What the Protagonist wants at the beginning may not be what she or he wants at the end, let alone what they need. Think of the number of romantic comedies that have one of the characters committed to another, only for the one – or both – to wind up in a clearly better relationship with someone else.

I also want to emphasize that both questions to be resolved are YES or NO questions. The Protagonists do not have to accomplish their goals; still less do they have to achieve their desires. In modern terms, a resolution in which the Protagonist gets what they truly need, as opposed to what they think they want, is a comedy (even if the tone is serious), and one in which they do not is a tragedy (even if the story has lots of laughs). You probably never realized that the story of Jack and Jill is a tragedy. There's no embarrassment in that; the person who first recited it to you probably didn't realize it either. Still, the fact that the poem ends with Jack and Jill still waterless makes it such.

One more word about the Resolution – it need not answer every possible question. Did Jack survive his injury? Did the relationship between Jack and Jill (whatever it was) survive the accident? *Was* it an accident? And will Flo or Doug or Jake show up to take care of the costs? Just a few of the questions to which answers we will never know. Unless, of course, we decide to make "Jack and Jill: The Series. . ."

An Allegory, and the Primary Question

An allegory that I've encountered repeatedly over the years helps me visualize the process. Incidentally, the authorship has been attributed to practically every famous writer, but as with Jack and Jill, the true creator has been lost to the mists of time. Whoever it may have been, though, the word "picture" is short and sweet:

Act I: Get your Protagonist(s) up a tree.

Figure 2.1 shows just that.

FIGURE 2.1 The Protagonist Sitting in a Tree.

26 The Story

In fact, the "act" of the photo begins with our Protagonist already in the tree, further demonstrating the point; get your Setup finished as quick as you can.

Act II: Throw rocks at them – or spears, grenades, laser blasts, as apropos.

FIGURE 2.2 The Antagonist Throwing Rocks at the Protagonist in the Tree.

FIGURE 2.3 The Protagonist Lying Underneath a Tree.

"As apropos" is key here. As shown in Figure 2.2, our Protagonist is so obvious, and our tree is so simple that an equally straightforward rock-throwing Antagonist is sufficient.

Act III: Get them down, one way or another – dead or alive, in fact – but get them down.

Granted, as shown in Figure 2.3, it looks like our Protagonist came down in a most unfortunate fashion, there is some ambiguity to the pose. (To paraphrase the ship's doctor of the starship mentioned above, "She's NOT dead, Jim!") Nevertheless, she is down. Whether there is room for a sequel to this tragedy is the point of the ambiguity.

The Second Primary Question

Behind the allegory, behind all our discussion so far, in fact behind every story ever told, is a question that was bestowed to me from my own mentor, Dr. Stuart Kaminsky. If you ever were blessed to take one of his writing classes, you and I both heard this question until we were more than ready never to hear it again. But he was right; it's the primary, in fact the ultimate, question for every storyteller:

Why Should I Care?

Why should I care? Why should I, the reader, care about your Setting, and your Conflict, and especially about your Characters? Why. Should. I. Care?

Answering that question is both the hardest and the most satisfying task for any writer. The guidelines in this chapter should prove most helpful to doing so. In our case as scriptwriters, the question is doubled – for while the viewers are our ultimate audience for our story, they are not our primary audience. The primary audience is the subject of the next chapter.

Works Cited

Cialdini, Robert B. *Influence: The Psychology of Persuasion*. Rev. ed., HarperCollins, 2007.

Koch, H. *Casablanca: Script and Legend*. The Overlook Press, 1992.

O'Rourke, P. J., *The Funny Stuff*. Edited by Terry McDonell, Atlantic Monthly Press, 2022.

Straczynski, J. M. *The Complete Book of Scriptwriting*. Rev. ed., Writers Digest Books, 2002.

3
THE PRODUCTION TEAM

The Target for the Script

Aiming at the Right Target: The Actual Readers of Your Script

If this were purely a work on story-writing, and especially if this were about novel-writing, I could inspire you with the dream of topping the bestseller lists, with millions of devoted fans perusing your page-turners. I might even hint that you could be the next Austen or Cervantes, attracting new generations of readers over decades or even centuries. In fact, you may indeed have talent comparable to the greats of the past; I certainly have no way of knowing otherwise.

However, this is a work on screenwriting. That being the case, no matter how much talent you possess, you are not going to have millions of readers. Your readership will, on the high side, be measured in round dozens. Further, you are extremely unlikely to be read over generations; more likely, your readers will be done with your work in a matter of months or possibly days.

That is because, no matter how successful your story is, your final audience will be watching and listening, not reading. Yet for that to happen, a very small readership over a short period of time will focus intently on the words you put on the page. Communicating clearly with that readership is the mark of the professional screenwriter, for that readership is your Production Team.

The Production Team is organized by the functions that each member fulfills to complete the project. While personnel titles vary somewhat between the different moving image media and the numerous countries in which they are produced, the team is traditionally broken down into the following departments:

- Producing, headed by the Producer
- Directing, headed by the Director

- Art, directed by the Production Designer
- Camera and its sub-departments, Electrical and Grip, headed by the Director of Photography
- Editorial and its adjunct department VFX, directed by the Editor
- Sound and Music, headed by the Sound Designer
- Cast, headed (more or less) by themselves

Reading this, you may be thinking, "There are more department heads listed than I have total crew!" Indeed, and this raises a very important point: *the functions of the whole team must be completed, even if the Team consists of one person. Someone* must do all these jobs to get the thing to the screens of your audience. Understanding what each part of the team does will improve your effectiveness as a writer, especially if you are working with a small team. The clearer you are from the beginning of the script, the surer the other members of the team will be in executing their roles, and the more the final project will resemble the vision you have in your head. That said, let us look at each department and its functions in turn.

The First Set of Readers: The Producing Department

The Producing Department's job is just that: to produce the project. The Producer guides the production from its inception to its final release; they are the head of all the business end, from development to distribution. Newcomers to the industry often confuse the Producer and the Director. A convenient way to think of the difference is the Director makes the video; the Producer makes the video happen.

This is shown in Figure 3.1 of a small production set.

The Producer, the woman standing in the photo, holds the essential tools of her trade; a copy of the Script; a walkie-talkie to communicate "in-house" with all of the crew; and a smartphone for, well, everything else. "Time is money" is a cliché in all 21st-century businesses, but in our business it's a cliché originating firmly and fully in reality. A production that is not setting up for a shot, getting a shot, or breaking down for a move to the next shot is still spending money. A key responsibility of the Producer, therefore, is to make setup, shot, and breakdown as efficient as possible, thus holding the production to two of the three fundamental documents of the project: the Budget and the Schedule. Her responsibility is multiplied because she created the Budget and the Schedule in the pre-production process. These two cornerstones are inextricably linked with each other and with the foundation of it all – the Script. We will therefore return to them in the next chapter as we discuss script structure.

Before we move on from the Producing Department, though, four terms that you will see in connection with it bear further discussion. First, on a

30 The Production Team

FIGURE 3.1 From Left to Right, the Producer, the Cast/Talent, the Director, and the Cinematographer.

large production, the Producer will have a team working under them. In that team, one often-confused item is the distinction between the Producer and the Line Producer. Most often seen on larger productions, the Producer is the head of the entire project, while the Line Producer oversees the nuts-and-bolts operation of a particular location or studio set. "I have numerous projects in various stages of development" is a well-known boilerplate statement of all Producers; for the most successful ones, it's usually true. The Line Producer is the essential proxy for the Producer on whichever project is in the stage of actual shooting. A Line Producer is especially useful on international productions. If you are shooting in a country other than your own, it is very helpful to have a Line Producer who knows the laws and customs of your host nation.

The title of Associate Producer is seen equally often on large productions. Unlike the Line Producer, this term is much more flexible. Associate Producers may be "fixers" as efficient – though more lawful – as Mr. Wolf in Quentin Tarantino's *Pulp Fiction* or consiglieres as insightful – though again more lawful – as Mr. Hagen from Francis Ford Coppola's *The Godfather*. On the other hand, they may also be people who began the production in much less glamorous jobs but with whom the Star has become enamored and for whom the Star is now demanding a more substantial role or at least paycheck. Associate Producer is often the title granted to these fortunate few. Since many of these latter have justified their patron's faith in them with considerable success, any rumors as to "who's who" may be dismissed as probably unkind and certainly unwise.

In streaming, cable, and broadcast series, two more Producing Department titles commonly pop up: the Creator and the Showrunner. The Creator is just that: the person who created the series in question. Unlike most features, the Creator is usually the writer as well, at the least of the pilot and the guide to the whole show, the series "bible." The Creator often authors additional episodes as well. For example, Rod Serling wrote almost half of the original *The Twilight Zone* science-fiction/fantasy anthology series; more recently, Charlie Brooker has written the majority of the not-dissimilar *Black Mirror*. The Showrunner is also a self-explanatory title; they run all the episodes of the show. Quite often, the Creator is also the Showrunner until another show gets picked up, at which point they hand off the show to a new Showrunner.

Regardless of their title, though, a point bears emphasis. The Producer will be one of the first two people, and one of the most important two people, who will read your script. It follows that one of the primary jobs of the screenwriter is to convey to the Producer all the information that they will need to "make the project happen" – all the details that must be known for budgeting and scheduling. Just so, the other primary job is to give the other most important person the details needed for all their decisions. That other most important person, the person who "makes the project," is of course the Director.

The Other First Set of Readers: The Directing Department

Much has been written about the balance of power between the Producer and the Director. In series projects, that balance is decidedly on the side of the Producer. The Director is making one episode; the Producer is making that episode; and all the rest of them happen. On the other hand, in single-unit productions such as features, the Director sees the balance shift more toward their side. Circumstances vary, of course. If you are a Director, your Producer's last name is Spielberg or Winfrey or Feige or Kennedy, and your last name is not – or not equally renowned – you will find yourself at something of a power disadvantage. Still, the Director is responsible for all the artistic decisions necessary for the project, even or especially if that brings them into conflict with the Producer. Your Director will read your script with those decisions in mind.

The pose in Figure 3.1 of the individualistic artist envisioning the scene through an improvised frame of thumbs and forefingers may seem somewhat stereotypical, but it is a stereotype based in the reality of the Director. Since they are being held responsible for the artistic vision, that is what they care about. In fact, the creative concept of the Director is perhaps even more important in short-form, micro-budget projects than in mammoth productions. When every dollar spent and every second of screen time is precious, the impact of each must be precisely directed.

As with the Producer, the Director also has a team working under them. In fact, their team is the largest team on the project; *all* creative departments and their heads ultimately answer to the Director. This underscores the importance of your script to the Director, and vice versa. Just as the Director will be reading your script for creative guidance, they will be interpreting your script as they give creative guidance to the various other creative talent. The reason that the Cast (aka Talent) is on the floor, the Cinematographer is on his haunches, the Director is framing the shot, and the Producer is looking on with a "hurry up" expression is because your script put them there.

In addition, the Director will have a smaller, specialized team known as the Directing Department, to whom your screenplay will also be crucial. The Casting Director will rely upon your script when working with the Director and the Producer to bring the Actors needed into the project. The Location Manager will scour the earth, or that part of it within the Budget, for the locations described in your screenplay. Finally, the Script Supervisor or Continuity Supervisor will come to know your script as intimately as you do. These unsung heroes (very informally known as "Scriptys") ensure, first, that the Director gets every needed shot from the script; second, that every shot matches the one before and after. The Scripty will thus be going back and forth between the Director, your script, and the other on-set departments.

Figures 3.2 and 3.3 show the importance of this position.

In the first, wider shot, our Protagonist holds a hand of poker, not a natural winner either. In the second shot, we see a CU of the Protagonist's hand. It's the Scripty's job to catch the (at least) five differences between the first shot and the second one and communicate them all to the Director. The Director must then decide whether or not to live with the mistake. That is not likely in this case, but it is possible. (Type the words "continuity errors" and your favorite series or feature title into your search engine for a quick idea of how often this happens.) If the Director decides not to live with it, it's their responsibility to set up new shots to fix the error. This will first involve, in this case, the Art Department.

The Readers to See What You See: The Art Department

In one of several confusing bits of production terminology, the Art Department is directed not by an Art Director but by the Production Designer. The

FIGURE 3.2 A Medium Shot (MS) of a Woman Holding a Hand of Cards.

FIGURE 3.3 A Close-Up (CU) of a Slightly Different Hand of Cards.

Production Designer is responsible to the Director for the entire visual look of the project. Every inanimate thing that is seen on screen was either placed there or left there by their conscious choice.

Those things can be broadly organized into four areas: sets; props; costumes, hair, and makeup; and special effects. If an actor steps onto a location and is photographed there, that location is a set. If an actor uses an object on camera, that object is a prop, no matter how small the object – as in the illustration above, where each card is a separate prop. If an actor wears it on camera, it's a costume, a hairdo, or a makeup job. Finally, if an actor is photographed with a visual effect that really exists in the physical world, but that was created especially for the production, it is a special effect.

Your screenplay will be the source material from which the Production Designer creates all sets, props, costumes, and special effects. We will go much deeper into the details of scene descriptions momentarily. For now, a simple guideline will suffice; if it is essential for your story for the Production Designer to get the set, prop, costume, or effect on camera, it is essential for your script that you write it.

Here's a simple example. The scene you imagine is a grumpy-but-loveable professor writing on a chalkboard with a yellow piece of chalk. You write, "Professor Curmudgeon writes his name, then turns to the class." The final edit shows good old Prof. C. writing on a whiteboard with a red dry-erase marker. The Production Designer took your details, or lack thereof, and created the visuals with the Director. You didn't write it; you are highly unlikely to see it.

Again, on a large production, there will be a large team of creative personnel to bring the vision of your screenplay, the Production Designer, and the Director to life. Crews will build entire sets for locations that never existed in real life; even more astonishing, they can and will redecorate entire real-world locations for the production, then put them back exactly as they were for the owners. Costumes are designed and specifically tailored for every cast member, as is hair and makeup. (A parenthetical note: a professional makeup artist once told me the best makeup jobs are not the science-fiction/fantasy/superhero transformations that usually get the nominations and always get the audience's attention. Rather, they're the ones the audience never notices; in her words, "Making an actress who's pushing forty look like she's mid-twenties is the real art.") The standard urban-drama shot of a taxi rolling down a midnight street as steam billows from a manhole – that steam is not a coincidence; the effects department put it there on cue. Props are custom-built for every situation in the script. And once again you may be saying, "My sets are where people will let me shoot, my props are what I can scrounge, my costumes are what my actors are wearing, and my effects are nonexistent. What does all this big-budget talk have to do with me?"

Just two things. First, creativity goes a long way, and part of that creativity involves writing to the budget – more about that later. Second, and even more important, there are two positions on a production on which you dare not cut corners; for which, if you choose to use them, you must spend what it takes to get the best pros available; and about which I am happy to stand on my soapbox and scream to the stars to get the point across. One of these positions we will discuss when we reach Cast. The other is the Armorer.

An Armorer is also known as a Weapons Master, Weapons Specialist, Weapons Coordinator, or Weapons Wrangler. As should be obvious, they are a props technician specializing in weapons, especially though not exclusively firearms. In the state of California, they require a special license. I believe they should have even more stringent licensing, and in every state in the United States and around the world as well.

Figure 3.4 illustrates why. As you can see, productions may call for handguns or shoulder arms. Within those broad categories, handguns may be semi-automatics, revolvers, single-shot "hunting handguns," or pocket derringers. Shoulder arms may be rifles or shotguns, either of which might be single shot, double barreled, pump action, lever action, bolt action, or semi-automatic. The production might call for any of the historical weapons shown or from even more eras besides. And this photo does not even include any fully automatic "machine gun" firearms, which are almost always required on modern action pictures. This bewildering array emphasizes the point: regardless of legal minimums, *the Armorer must be expert at the safe handling of all weapons used on the production, firearms, or any other type.* Now then: this

FIGURE 3.4 A Collection of Firearms Illustrating that of a Professional Armorer.

text is designed to show you how to write what you want to write, not tell you what to write or not. But in this case, I make an exception.

There is nothing, nothing, nothing that is higher priority on set than cast and crew safety. So, if you know that you are writing for a production that cannot afford a competent Armorer, and you have written any kind of weapon use into your script – **CUT IT**. Even if the weapon is only to be shown, not actually used – unless, of course, the budget does allow for a realistic but entirely nonfunctional model of said weapon. As the tragic and, as of this writing, still legally unresolved death of Halyna Hutchins on the set of the feature *Rust* illustrates all too well, we media Producers must not compromise on this point. I repeat; *if you can't afford the Armorer, don't write the weapon.*

Enough said, I hope. And, also, this wraps the discussion of the Art Department. So far, almost everything we have discussed we hold in common with our artistic kin in theater. Now we move into those departments that set us apart from our stage friends.

The Readers to See How You See: The Camera Department

The Camera Department also includes two subordinate departments, Electrical and Grip. Just as the Art Department under the Production Designer is responsible for everything that goes in front of the camera, the Camera Department under the Director of Photography (generally abbreviated DP in the United States, DOP in the United Kingdom) is responsible for everything that goes into the camera and onto the recording medium. So much is obvious. What is not obvious is the DP may never actually touch the camera on a studio feature or network series. Some do, of course, and the title Cinematographer is generally, though not universally, used when the DP operates their own camera. Figure 3.1 illustrates this; as the Talent settles in, the Cinematographer is preparing to get his own shot. However, the DP is quite often the head of a team, which also includes the Camera Operator, the First AC, and the Second AC.

Camera Operator is self-explanatory. First AC stands for First Assistant Camera. One of the First AC's primary responsibilities is the care and maintenance of the camera. The other is described in the alternate title, the Focus Puller. On a professional production, the "point-and-shoot", "run-and-gun," smartphone-video style simply will not produce the desired photographic results. This is especially true when it comes to focus. Before each shot, the Focus Puller will carefully measure the distance between the camera and every essential focal point in the take, as shown in Figure 3.5.

They will then mark the measured distance on the camera control known as the follow focus wheel. As the shot progresses, the Camera Operator will move the camera to keep the subject properly framed, while the Focus Puller

FIGURE 3.5 A First AC/Focus Puller Taking a Measurement from Camera to Subject Prior to a Shot.

turns the follow focus wheel to the correct marked distance to keep the subject in focus. If this sounds like a complicated dance to keep in step during even a modestly complex shot, it is. That's why Camera Ops and 1st ACs get paid.

Their teammate, the Second AC, is not directly involved in this dance. Their steps occur immediately before and after the shot. The 2nd AC is also known as the Clapper Loader. Their first responsibility is to load whatever medium the camera uses to record the image and, when said medium is full, to unload it and get it safely to the editing team. This process is considerably more challenging when the medium in question is film, as opposed to digital; but as anyone who's ever taken a shot with no SD card in the camera will testify, it's equally crucial in all media.

The second responsibility is to operate the clapper, also known as the slate, clapboard, or board. Most movie fans will recognize this as the black-and-white board with the hinged pieces of wood that "claps" in almost any movie about moviemaking, and which has entered pop culture as a symbol of filmmaking on everything from jewelry to wall art. What fans may not realize is that the look and sound of the clap is more than just a cool effect, just as the information on the board itself is more than window dressing.

Since motion pictures recorded the image on film and the sound on other media (first wax, later magnetic tape), there had to be a way to synchronize

FIGURE 3.6 A 2nd AC/Clapper Loader Preparing to Operate the Clapboard Prior to a Shot.

the sound and the picture. To oversimplify a bit, the editor lined up the visual frame in which the two pieces met with the sound of the clap. Once those were aligned, all the rest of the sound would be perfectly in sync. The information on the slate, meanwhile, told the editor all they needed to know about what they were watching and hearing: scene number, shot number, take number, Director, DP, and, of course, the production itself. Nowadays, the slate is much more likely to be a whiteboard, as shown in Figure 3.6. Budget allowing, it will also have a digital display for video time code. As with so many other things, there are also downloadable apps for tablets or even smartphones that turn them into fully functional clappers. Regardless of the device used, the information and synchronization, though, are even more crucial today than in the Golden Age. The digital age has made it easier to shoot and edit more footage, which means that more footage is shot to be edited, which in turn means that organization based on the clapper's information is even more time-saving. Of course, there are a plethora of cameras that record sound and picture; still, most professional productions use the camera only for image, while recording the audio separately on a dedicated digital recorder. The need for the slate, therefore, still stands.

Three more specialists in camera operation bear mention. The first is the stabilizer system operator, better known as the Steadicam operator. Steadicam was the first such system, which like Kleenex or Xerox has become the standard term for all such systems. Regardless of manufacturer, the stabilizer system is a reinforced vest worn by the operator with a motion-isolating arm attached, to which the camera is mounted. In short, camera and operator become one flowing unit.

The opposite of this, in some ways, is the motion control operator. The motion control unit is a robotic mount that is programmed to precisely repeat camera movement as many times as needed. The motion control unit has become crucial in the age of Computer-Generated Imagery (CGI). Since the focal length, framing, movement, and so forth of the computer viewpoint never vary, the camera photographing the real actors cannot change either. Thus, the operator programs the unit to match the CGI sequences.

Advances in technology have put systems that mimic the Steadicam within financial reach of many productions; not so motion control units. On the other hand, affordability, capability, and licensing requirements for the third camera specialty, the drone operator, have practically made it a new base requirement for production. Aerial drones have taken camera movement to new heights, pun fully intended.

Whether you're shooting from a drone, a Steadicam, a motion control arm, or a plain old tripod, though, the Camera team's procedure remains the same. The 2nd AC loads the camera and prepares the clapper, as the Camera Op and the 1st AC prepare the shot. The 2nd AC operates the slate, and the Camera Op and the 1st AC take the shot. The 2nd AC makes notes about the shot and, when the medium is full, has notes and medium delivered to the editor. Now, you may be asking, "If the team did all that, what did the DP do?"

The DP *directed* their teammates. Every aspect of the shot was the DP's choice, working from their knowledge of their camera itself, the medium on which they are shooting, the mount in use, and the lenses available. Furthermore, while their Camera team was setting up the camera itself, the DP was also directing the Electrical and Grip team in the other half of the shot – the lighting.

First-time visitors to a professional set or studio are almost always shocked at the complexity of the lighting setups and the number of lights used to achieve them. This is especially true when said guests are fans of an existing show; the light that looks so natural on the home screen takes such effort to achieve. Indeed, it can be said that few parts of our industry work as hard to not be noticed. Whether the results are naturalistic or dramatic, though, an equal amount of effort and expertise are essential.

That effort is divided between the Electrical and the Grip Departments. The Electrical Department is headed by the Gaffer. They design and plan the efficient and safe operation of all lighting and its power source to achieve the effect desired by the DP. Given that all these lights draw impressive electrical current loads that may involve tapping directly into main power conduits and operating multiple generators, the necessity for expertise is obvious. (Incidentally, the term "gaffer" may originate from an archaic term for "grandfather" or "godfather," a British slang term for a job foreman, the long pole with hooked end called a "gaff" that was once the primary equipment used for lights, or almost anything else one could think of – its precise beginning has been lost to the mists of time.)

The Grip Department, headed by the Key Grip, sets up all lights and other production equipment according to the Gaffer's plan. As shown in Figure 3.7, once again, on smaller productions one person can fulfill both Gaffer and Key Grip roles.

A specialist on this team merits particular explanation. The Dolly Grip sets up and operates the dolly, the wheeled platform that carries the camera, the tripod, the Camera Op and sometimes the Director for camera moves that require such. In other words, the Dolly Grip pushes the dolly, camera, tripod, and one or two people back and forth as many times as necessary to get a usable take. If that sounds very much like hard work, it is; they and the Steadicam operators are usually some of the fittest people on a set.

One final member of the Camera Department also deserves mention.

The Production Sound Technician, as seen in Figure 3.8, is responsible for recording the best sound possible on all locations, sets, and studios. An experienced sound tech's expertise in microphone choice and placement is equal to the DP's knowledge of lenses and filters, and equally important to the final production. While projects with moderate-to-extravagant budgets can access the facilities and expertise to replace the actors' lines that were lost to misfortune (a process called ADR, for Automated Dialogue Replacement), every Producer would rather spend the money on something else. Further, in my experience, as great as the ADR might be, it never beats the original performance.

That last thought should be your focus, if you are reading these words and thinking "I've got one person to run the camera and one to hold the boom pole the mic's on." As with production design, camera work is a matter of inspiration over remuneration. You may indeed have to adapt your vision to your resources; but if you articulate that vision clearly, it can be clearly conveyed to screen by your DP/cinematographer/videographer.

"So how do I do *that?*" I promise, we're getting there . . . as soon as we address the closely related production departments whose work is revving up as everyone else is winding down.

The Readers to See the Order You See: The Editorial Department

So, everything has been shot, recorded, captured, "in the can" to use the expression from the days of actual shooting on film. You doubtless know that practically no production of any significance is shot in one shot. You

FIGURE 3.7 A Crew Member Working as Both Gaffer and Key Grip Adjusting a Light.

FIGURE 3.8 A Production Sound Technician Prepares to Record Audio.

probably also know that practically no production of any significance is shot in the order that the audience sees the shots on screen. And you certainly know that no production of any significance gets the perfect shot on the first take every time, or possibly any time. Someone must gather all those takes of all those shots and organize them for the most efficient selection. Someone must select the best takes, assemble them into a coherent whole, and ensure that each take visually fits with the one before and the one after. In short, someone must edit the piece, and that someone is the Editor.

The development of the Editor's technology is a fascinating history, but for good or ill, it is simply history at this point. It might almost be said that modern video production has evolved into a circle. It begins with a person (you the Screenwriter) sitting in front of a computer, and it ends with a person (the Editor, possibly also you) sitting in front of a computer. Regardless of what the project is shot on – and the number of projects shot on film gets smaller every year – it will be edited on computer, using any of a variety of digital nonlinear editing (DNLE) systems. Editors are thus not only masters of the editing craft, they are experts in the operation of their computer systems. The Assistant Editor is also a computer expert; in addition to their roles as apprentices learning from the editor, they are responsible for getting material into and out of the computer. On many contemporary productions, from features to commercials, the third vital member of the team is the VFX Supervisor. VFX equals Visual Effects, including and especially those created with CGI. As sitting through the credits of any summer blockbuster shows, a full discussion of the people and techniques involved in all facets of VFX and CGI would easily be a book on its own. Thus, we move on to the production department working hand in hand with the Editor.

The Readers to Hear What You Hear: The Sound and Music Department

As the Editor is editing the picture, the Sound Designer is creating the soundtrack. Once again, on larger productions the Sound Designer will direct a team of specialists to handle the different aspects of audio. A Dialogue Editor edits all the actors' speech; a Music Editor edits all music; and a Sound Editor edits all sound effects – that is, everything neither dialogue nor music that's heard in the production. Those sounds are largely the work of a specialist called a Foley artist, who recreates the sounds of everything from footsteps to forest fires in a specialized studio. Digital synthesizers have taken on some of this work, of course. In another consequence of the digital age, the Editor may also be the Sound Designer; in other words, one person often edits both video and audio for the production, and on the same machine. The flexibility and capability of 21st-century computers have made this merger possible with fewer drawbacks than even just a few years ago.

Finally, there is the "department" that stands by itself, to the point that they are not usually listed as such. Nonetheless, no other people on the production will spend more time with your script than they will. That is, of course...

The Readers to Say and Do What You Hear and See: The Cast

If, as I said in Chapter 2, "All stories are about individual people," then the individual people who say the lines and do the actions that we write for them are the lifeblood of our stories. There is a stereotype that some of them are all too aware of this. That does not change the fact that if your actors cannot connect with the dialogue and directions, the production is lost.

Once again, you may be thinking that professional on-camera talent is beyond your budget. For full-time professional actors, that may indeed be the case. For performers with talent, on the other hand, not necessarily. If you have any community theater in your area, you may be pleasantly surprised at the variety and level of performers who are willing to work with your budget. Further, even if they can't fit your production schedule into their lives, they will almost certainly be able to give you a table read. Simply hearing other people really say the lines you wrote will go a long way toward determining if, to paraphrase Harrison Ford's legendary words to George Lucas on the set of the original *Star Wars*, you have typed (ahem) guano that is in fact impossible to say.

Another point on the cast should be highlighted because it's so easily overlooked by beginning and less-affluent media creators. Think back to our friends from the commercials of the previous chapter. Now consider how many times Flo or Jake or Doug or Mayhem interact with crowds of people, none of whom speak in the commercial. Those people are played by background actors or extras. I prefer the first term because the illusion of realism that they create is nearly as important as the performances of the leading players. Even a low-budget production can usually scrounge up people to be café patrons or sports spectators, within reason. Free pizza and T-shirts can work wonders.

Finally, the final Cast specialty discussion should give you a sense of déjà vu. As with the Armorer, so there is one position in the Cast on which you dare not cut corners – for which, if you choose to use them, you must spend what it takes to get the best pros available and about which I am happy to stand on my soapbox and scream to the stars to get the point across. If you have a fight scene more intense than a pillow fight, a driving scene with anything other than the legal and safe standards for everyday motorists, a fall more challenging than a flop onto a feather bed – *if you have any sort of "action" in your script, you must employ the properly trained AND equipped Stunt Performers.* As I said earlier, this text is designed to show you how to write what you want to write, not tell you what to write or not. But again, in this case, I make an exception.

There is nothing, nothing, nothing that is higher priority on set than cast and crew safety. So, if you know that you are writing for a production that cannot afford competent Stunt Performers, and you have written any kind of Stunt into your script – CUT IT. This may mark a time that you as a Producer/Director have to say a very firm "NO" to your Cast. An actress who has earned her black belt is doubtless well trained in that martial art, but it is not the same skill as Stunt fighting. She may also enjoy legal auto racing through an organization like the Sports Car Club of America, but that is not the same skill as Stunt driving. When you are the Showrunner, NEVER let a performer not specifically trained in Stunts persuade you that "they can handle it." We media Producers must not compromise on this point. I repeat, *if you can't afford the Stunt Performer, don't write the Stunt.*

The Primary Question, and the Other Primary Question

That brings us to the primary question, and the *other* primary question, with which to end this concise overview of production. The primary question is, "***Does my script give all these artists the information they need to bring the project to life?***" As I hope I made clear, that is a lot of information. Knowing who does what, and something of how they do it, is the first step toward giving them what they need to do it. The rest of our time together is devoted to the specifics of how.

The other primary question is one I've hinted at throughout this chapter. In terms of emotional impact, it may be the first query. That question is, "***What if all these people are me?***" Here I'm afraid I have good news and bad news.

The bad news first: other than you, ***no one cares if all these people are you.*** By that I mean; if you are going to style yourself a professional – in other words, if you hope to get paid for all this – you are going to be judged against the work of other professionals. You may indeed be Producer/Director/Production Designer/Videographer/Editor/Sound Designer and "Star." I don't necessarily recommend it; but if you are, your audience is comparing your work to Netflix, or the BBC, or Univision, or any of the Disney conglomerate – *if* you want to be a professional. Actually, I must go further. If you want to *consistently* reach an audience that is drinking from the firehose of content from all the media Producers of the world, you've got to compete on their quality level. That may not seem fair, but to quote the dean of screenwriters, William Goldman, "Who says life is fair? Where is that written?" (339).

Now the good news. You can survive that comparison. That largely depends on you, and your professionalism as a screenwriter. I don't know your talent level, your IQ, your work ethic, your emotional stability, or any of the other qualities of you. I do know how you can hone your professional approach on any budget level. The foundation of this is the subject of the next chapter.

Works Cited

Goldman, William. *Four Screenplays*. Applause Theatre & Cinema Books, 1995.

4

THE FORMAT

The Structure of the Script

The Script as Score and Blueprint

Like a lot of Americans of my generation, I took piano lessons as a kid. Like a lot of my fellow music students, it was my parents' idea, and I got away from it at an early opportunity. Like a lot of my peers, I've regretted that childish decision – a lot. One thing that has remained from those long-gone days, though, is the image of a page of music. I am no expert, but I can still distinguish a treble clef from a bass clef and a whole note from a half-note in modern notation. If Providence had gifted me a different set of talents and aspirations, and I was writing Broadway scores instead of screenwriting texts, I would have to know the modern music notation system inside out. A Broadway composer whose music cannot be read by musicians, singers, and conductors obviously is no Broadway composer; in fact, they are not a composer at all. Even worse, perhaps, would be the composer whose notations almost express what they have in their imagination. How frustrating would it be to hear the conductor cue the orchestra and the singers, and the burst of music nearly matches what you heard in your head – but not quite, and you have no way of communicating what to change.

Now, my musical byways are many miles in the rear-view mirror, but one career highway that I never even glanced down is engineering. Fortunately for this illustration, one of my best friends is an engineer. He has often regaled me with the importance of properly creating and labeling schematic drawings for a project. Frustrating as the creative limitations would be in music, there's an even more practical frustration in the engineering world – spending thousands of dollars on building parts that almost function but actually malfunction. An engineer who regularly submitted such schematics will no longer be an engineer, at least an employed one.

I bring in these two disparate fields because creating a moving image production is an art, like making music. It also has numerous technical aspects with financial implications, like engineering. For these reasons, like both music and engineering, screenwriting has rules that govern how the project in the writer's imagination must be committed to paper or computer file. These rules are summed up in the concept of format.

For those of us who fell in love with reading as kids, and especially those of us who thus discovered a love of creative writing, the "format" for novels and short stories is probably second nature. Those of us who also discovered a love of theater are also familiar with the format of stage plays. Once again, I have good news and other news. The good news: the formats of moving image production are no more difficult to learn than that of the stage. The other news: as implied in the previous sentence, there are multiple formats.

The first format we will discuss is variously called the narrative format, the narrative film format, the film-style format, or simply the screenplay format. It was developed in the Golden Age of Hollywood, as *The Jazz Singer* catapulted the medium from "silents" to sound. Two factors led to its quick standardization. The first was the geographic centralization of the eight major motion picture studios in the Los Angeles area. The second and possibly more important was formation of the Motion Pictures Producers and Distributors of America (MPPDA). The MPPDA, which evolved into the Motion Pictures Association of America (MPAA) and then into today's Motion Pictures Association (MPA), formalized the economic intertwining of the major studios and the entire American movie industry. This financial interdependence sped the adoption of the new script standard. Since, for a variety of reasons, the United States industry was already dominating the global business, it spread internationally as well.

Today, the narrative screenplay format is the core of all entertainment scripts that are designed to be shot single camera. It also is used as a foundation for high-end commercial production. Perhaps most important to the writer, it is the default format for every screenwriting software of which I'm aware. If you aspire to the entertainment world, I recommend investing in one of these software packages. There are numerous alternatives with various price points; you should have little difficulty finding the right one for your style and budget.

However, it is perfectly possible to write a professional format screenplay without investing in any software. After all, screenwriters were hammering out features for roughly fifty years before word processors were even invented. Just as there are a variety of software programs that will auto-format your screenplay, so there are numerous texts with instructions to use the average word processing program to properly format a script. And as noted, the basics are hardly "rocket surgery or brain science," as illustrated in the following two short scenes.

```
INT. JACK AND JILL COTTAGE - DAY
JACK, a sturdy, clean-cut lad, and JILL, an athletic,
adventurous young woman, smile at each other in their neat and
cheerful one-room home.

                    JACK
          Today's the day!

                    JILL
               (kisses Jack)
          I can't wait!

They shoulder their backpacks; Jack gallantly opens the door for
Jill, and she precedes him outside.

EXT. VILLAGE-TO-HILL ROAD - DAY
Jill and Jack step out of their small yard onto the path that
leads to the hill in the distance. With another exchanged smile,
they stride off into the rising sun.
```

These few lines contain all the basic elements of the screenplay.

Narrative Screenplay Element 1: The Header

The first line of each scene is the *Header*, also called the *scene heading* or *slugline*. From the example above:

```
INT. JACK AND JILL COTTAGE - DAY
```

Every new scene in the script must begin with one of these. The header itself has three components, two of which are straightforward. The first, INT or EXT, tells the reader whether the scene takes place inside, in an INTERIOR, or outside, in an EXTERIOR. As a rule, if there's a roof overhead, it's an Interior; if not, Exterior. The last component is the time of day. You have some flexibility here as to how specific the time need be, but I recommend beginning writers keep it simple. If the sun is up, even partially, write it as DAY; if the sun is down, NIGHT. You can get more specific if needed in the scene description, as I did above.

The middle component of the header is the one with practically infinite variations. That is the *Location*, where your scene takes place. This is limited only by your imagination. There are three guidelines to keep in mind as you commit your imagination to text here, though. Locations must be *clear*, *concise*, and *consistent*.

Clear. In the example above, Jill and Jack have a one room home – a studio cottage, so to speak. Thus, INT. COTTAGE is sufficient to state where our cast and crew will be shooting this opening scene. If they resided in J&J Manor, I would have added the area in said mansion, such as INT. J&J MANOR FOYER. Even if they owned a typical house in a typical suburb, I would have specified the room: INT. J&J HOME KITCHEN. I make that point because I often read novice scripts that say INT. J&J HOUSE, forgetting that most houses have more than one room. Your production crew needs to know specifically where to set up; the header must tell them clearly. As I noted in Chapter 3, if it isn't in the script at all, it most likely won't happen; if it isn't in the script clearly, it most likely will happen wrongly.

The practical demands of production demand a balance between specificity and generics in the header, though. Let's say a script begins with INT. OFFICE. There are all kinds of offices in the world, and many of them may be available for the production. This has the advantage of giving your Producer lots of flexibility – too much flexibility. Lawyers, doctors, professors, CEOs, and dozens more occupations have offices, and each has its own unique aspects. The one the Producer secures might be totally unsuited for the project and will almost certainly be totally unlike what you envision. On the other hand, if you know that your scene *must* take place in one place on Earth, and that place only, it's acceptable to name it in your header. For example, if it were essential that your scene take place in the office of the President of the United States, you could write INT. OVAL OFFICE. This is certainly specific, and everyone involved in the production knows precisely where they will be. The drawback: this places an extra burden on the Producing team. They must secure that location – or pay for building a duplicate set – or the script cannot be produced as envisioned. And that will certainly come back on you.

One other word about Location: it may include time as well as place. If you are writing a script that moves back and forth between years, or if you are writing a script that takes place entirely in the past of currently existing places, you may add the year to the location. For example,

```
INT. BUCKINGHAM PALACE STATE ROOM, 1798 – DAY
```

to distinguish from

```
INT. BUCKINGHAM PALACE STATE ROOM, 2023 – DAY.
```

It might be necessary to go beyond year to date or even time, but those are usually more easily dealt with in descriptions.

To sum up: the Location must be clear, specific enough to convey the essentials of the scene, and generic enough to meet the practical needs of production.

Concise. Regardless of whether your Location name leans toward flexibility or precision, it must be short. The rule, and this is as close as we come to a strict rule on this subject, is that the entire Header must fit on one line. If it doesn't, shorten it. Abbreviations are fine so long as everyone on the Production Team understands them. And that's that for conciseness.

Consistent. Finally, once you have created a Location term, use the identical term every time the same location is meant. I cannot overstress this point. The Header is the key element of the screenplay for the Producer, as far as organization of the Schedule and creation of the Budget is concerned. It is crucial that, as I stated above, you begin every new scene of the screenplay with a new header. If you go from inside a shed to outside it, those are two: the first,

```
INT. SHED - DAY
```

the second,

```
EXT. SHED - DAY.
```

If the next scene is outside the shed at night, you go from

```
EXT. SHED - DAY
```

to

```
EXT. SHED - NIGHT.
```

Of course, if you go from the shed to some other place, that too is a scene change because of the different Location.

When organizing the production, the Producer seeks to schedule all EXT DAY scenes together, all EXT NIGHT scenes, all INT NIGHT, and all INT DAY. Within these groups, the Producer will put all scenes in the same Location together – which is why consistency is so important. The foyer of Jack and Jill's palatial estate must not be J&J MANOR FOYER on page 1, J&J MANOR HALL a few pages later, J&J MANSION ENTRYWAY later still. The rest of the production team has no idea that you mean the same place with all three phrases; as far as they are concerned, these are three *different* Locations. When it is discovered that you intended only one, once again that will certainly come back on you. So, it is J&J MANOR FOYER on page 1, page 10, page 100, page ad infinitum for every Header in which that Location is used. Once each Header is written comes the second element.

Narrative Screenplay Element 2: The Scene Description

Again, from the example above, the first scene description:

```
JACK, a sturdy, clean-cut lad, and JILL, an athletic,
adventurous young woman, smile at each other in their neat and
cheerful one-room home.
```

The scene description will be discussed at length in the next chapter. For now, it suffices to say that it roughly corresponds to the stage directions in a theatrical play. It tells us about the setting, characters, and action: where the Audience is looking into, who the Audience is looking at, and what the people whom the Audience is watching are doing. Still, three technical notes on the grammar of the scene bear note. First, the scene description in English is always written in third person. Second, it is always written in present tense. Third, it is almost always written in active voice. As in the example above, "They shoulder their backpacks." Most professional writing in English is in third person, so that needs no further explanation. On the other hand, most writing in English is in past tense, not present. The purpose of present tense in scene descriptions is to write each scene as if it is happening as you write it. Finally, active voice is also the usual English sentence structure. The only time you will give it extra thought is in the very rare exceptions, when it is the object, not the subject, that is the most important thing in the sentence.

Narrative Screenplay Element 3: The Dialogue

Just as there are a cornucopia of books about screenwriting in general, so there are a host of books about how to write dialogue – character conversation. In its simplest form, from the example above:

```
                    JACK
           Today's the day!

                    JILL
                (kisses Jack)
            I can't wait!
```

Personally, I do two things to improve my own dialogue. First, I read it aloud myself; then I enlist talented friends from my local theater scene for a table read. But before anyone can read it, it must be properly formatted into its three parts.

Two of these parts are essential. First, obviously, is the **Character Name**. What that will be has far too many factors to list, let alone elaborate. Still, there are three guidelines that can be useful across all genres and settings. First, I do not give characters the same, or similar-sounding, names unless I intend to make the name likeness a point of the plot. Second, I do strive to give every person who speaks a name. We have already discussed the relationship between name and character; beyond that, there are practical reasons to name your speakers. From the perspective of you as a writer, and from the perspectives of the Producer and the Director, it's easier to keep track of "Officer Smith" and "Officer Lopez" than "Cop #1" and "Cop #2." From the cast's perspective, any actor would rather play "Officer Lopez" than "Cop #1" for two reasons; as already stated, the names make them Characters, and practically speaking "Officer Lopez" looks much better than "Cop #1" in onscreen credits and actors' resumes. Third, once "Officer Smith" and "Officer Lopez" have been named, their names stay the same every time they speak. Their names are also the same the first time they appear in any scene description. The reason is the same as Location names; those Character Names are going to be organized into the Production Schedule, and different names mean different characters.

The second essential part of the Dialogue, even more obviously, is the *Dialogue* itself, also called the *Line* – what the character says. I won't attempt to condense all those tomes about how to write dialogue here, though we will discuss dialogue more in Chapter 8. One point, though, should be emphasized upfront. There is some controversy over the proper way to write accents and dialects, particularly those of less-privileged communities. My approach is to write the dialogue in "standard" English; indicate the relevant linguistic background of the character in the description; and leave it to the actor and the Director to work out the details of the performance. I especially recommend this approach if you are attempting to write the speech of a demographic of which you are not a member.

The third and last component of the Dialogue is not essential, and yet is often the one that gives beginning screenwriters the most trouble. That is the *Parenthetical*, which is a short phase inserted, in parentheses, between the Character Name and the Line. In the example above, (kisses Jack) is a Parenthetical. The reason it often trips up newcomers is the temptation to overuse it, especially to indicate how the writer thinks the dialogue should be said, and – for whatever reason – most especially if they think the line should be delivered "wryly," as in

```
                JACK
             (wryly)
        Today's the day!


                JILL
             (wryly)
        I can't wait!
```

That was so common at one point that professional screenwriters started calling Parentheticals for line delivery "Wrylies." The short rule is, don't write "Wrylies." Actors and Directors hate it; it intrudes on their work of shaping the performances themselves. Despite this overall prohibition, though, there are six circumstances in which parentheticals may be used properly.

Use Parentheticals for Voice-Overs

A *Voice-Over* is any time that the character's voice is heard by the audience, but the character is not physically speaking in the scene. It is quite common in documentaries, where an unseen narrator tells the audience additional information that they could not glean from the visuals – or, in worst cases, describes what the audience is seeing. In video fiction, it is a staple if not a cliché of film noir. The placement is a bit different from standard parentheticals, though; if you intend it in your script, it is indicated with (VO) placed immediately after the Character Name. For example:

```
          JILL (V.O.)
     I can't wait!
```

Use Parentheticals for Off-Screen

An *Off-Screen* line is any time that the character's voice is heard by the audience and the character is physically speaking in scene, but the character is not seen by the audience. For example, if your Protagonist is in their bedroom and hears someone calling from another room or from outside the house altogether, that is an Off-Screen line. As with Voice-Overs, the placement is a bit different from standard parentheticals, though; if you intend it in your script, it is indicated with (OS) placed immediately after the Character Name, just as with Voice-Overs.

```
          JILL (O.S.)
     I can't wait!
```

Use Parentheticals for Other Languages

This may come as a surprise, but if you want your characters to speak a language that you yourself do not speak, you do not need to first learn the language yourself. In fact, you need not even look up the translation. A line that needs to be delivered in any other language than English, or whatever language in which you are writing, can be designated with a simple parenthetical. It then becomes the responsibility of the Actor to learn how to say that line in that language. If you also want the line subtitled in the language of the production, that is indicated in the Scene Description.

```
                    JILL
                (in Elvish)
            I can't wait!
```

Use Parentheticals for Electronic Media

I was a disc jockey for my college radio station, and while I pursued other careers I never lost my affection for good audio. One thing I learned during my time on the air is that my voice sounded quite different on an air-check recording than it did in person. This in turn made me realize that every electronic medium affects its audio differently. If you want to specify this effect in your work, you may use a Parenthetical (Filtered), which tells the production team to apply the appropriate audio filter. Depending on the detail your Sound Designer requires, or will tolerate, you may add the specific medium on which the line is heard:

```
                    JILL
                (Filtered - FM Radio)
            I can't wait!
```

Use Parentheticals for Bits

A *brief* action that *must* be done while the Actor is delivering the line is known as a "Bit." These may be written in Parentheticals as well, but I emphasize "brief" and "must." Again, from the example above:

```
                    JILL
                (kisses Jack)
            I can't wait!
```

Jill's private display of affection here will be important enough to the full story for me to specify it here – at least it would be if I were writing the full script. To repeat: Actors and Directors want to work out the specifics of the performances themselves, and they highly resent the overuse of Bits. They especially resent it if the Bit is actually a Scene Description. All Parentheticals should be shorter than the Lines they precede, which means that it takes very few words to make a Parenthetical take up lots of space on the page. My rule is, if I must write a Bit and that Bit takes up more than two lines, it is a Scene Description and should be written as such.

Use Parentheticals for Delivery

A last word on the subject of Parentheticals:

Rarely, if you absolutely must, as a last resort, and if there is no way the actor and the Director, working together, could deduce the delivery in context, you may insert the manner a line should be said in a parenthetical. By "manner" I mostly mean "volume"; if a character begins speaking at a different level, for reasons not apparent from what's gone before, for example.

```
            JILL
         (whispers)
    I can't wait!
```

If you feel you need to insert the emotion of the line in the Parenthetical, it may be an indication you need to look at the clarity of your scene.

These are the basics of the narrative/film-style/screenplay format. As already mentioned, it is the foundational format for most entertainment video. It is also the default for scripts purchased by "Hollywood" Producers. For both those reasons, it *must* be followed precisely. If a Producer picks up your script, the first thing they will do is count the number of pages. In this format, the number of pages approximately equals the number of finished minutes of screen time. Further, for feature production, the number of pages also roughly equals the number of days of production. Broadcast, cable, and streaming series are produced more quickly, but similar calculations are done for them too. Thus, in the Producer's mind, your script of one hundred pages will require a hundred days of production (editing and other post-production not included). At the end of post-production, the completed feature should be a hundred minutes in length. If your format is off, all these calculations will be off. This will make the Producer unhappy, who will then make you, the writer, unhappy.

"But you've been saying throughout that this kind of screenwriting is not the focus of this book," you may be thinking. "Why all this time spent on this format?" Besides the reasons already noted, the primary motive is that the other format we'll discuss is largely adapted from the screenplay format. That format is called the two-column, the dual-column, or, most commonly, the split-column format.

Here a bit of history is in order. In the earliest days of television in the United States, there were only four networks: NBC, CBS, ABC, and Dumont. Dumont, sadly, was defunct by the mid-1950s, leaving only the so-called Big Three. Since all three were (and are) headquartered in New York City, one might expect that the TV industry would be even more centralized and thus standardized than the movie business. American television, though, is part of broadcasting and thus under the authority of the Federal Communication Commission (FCC). Among many other functions, the FCC regulates how many local stations may be owned by any one entity. The Big Three networks were allowed a few of those, and mostly chose to establish themselves in the top 3 markets of New York City, Los Angeles, and Chicago. These stations became known as "O&Os" because they were owned and operated directly by the networks. The rest of the more than 500 local stations on the air by 1960 had not quite as many owners as there were stations. Most of these others were affiliates of the networks; they contracted to carry network programming but weren't controlled by the net. A few others were completely independent of any network.

In short, FCC regulation led to the decentralization of control of the local stations of America. On top of this, the networks did not supply enough programming to fill a broadcast day, even for the O&Os. Therefore, in the Golden Age of Television, local stations produced many of their own shows. All this independent production led to much experimentation with different and possibly better ways to do things. That included scriptwriting, and from this came the *basic* split-column format.

I emphasize "basic" because all these independent experiments led to quite a few variations on the format. The example in Appendix 1 is from my own experience; as you proceed through your career, you will encounter differing details from others. The essential format is the same throughout, though, and that is the most important thing.

The split-column format embodies two revolutionarily simple ideas. First, each page of the script is split into two columns. The left column is labeled "Video." Everything that the audience can see goes in the Video column. The right column is labeled "Audio"; everything that the audience can hear *as they see what's in the Video* goes in the Audio column. Second, rather than breaking only between each scene, the split-column breaks between each shot. In other words, every time the audience's perspective on the action changes in your mind's eye, you create a new row of the script.

In this format, our intro scenes with Jack and Jill would look like this:

VIDEO	AUDIO
1. MLS - INT. JACK AND JILL COTTAGE - DAY	1. JACK: Today's the day!
JACK, a sturdy, clean-cut lad, and JILL, an athletic, adventurous young woman, smile at each other in their neat and cheerful one-room home.	
2. MCU - INT. JACK AND JILL COTTAGE - DAY	2. JILL: I can't wait!
JILL kisses JACK.	
3. MS - INT. JACK AND JILL COTTAGE - DAY They shoulder their backpacks; Jack gallantly opens the door for Jill, and she precedes him outside.	3. MUSIC: folk instrumental.

58 The Format

VIDEO	AUDIO
4. WS - EXT. VILLAGE-TO-HILL ROAD - DAY Jill and Jack step out of their small yard onto the path that leads to the hill in the distance. With another exchanged smile, they stride off into the rising sun.	4. MUSIC: folk instrumental CONTINUES.

In this format, while conciseness is still a Header objective, the one-line-per-location rule is not in force. The first reason is that we have only half a line with which to work. The second reason is that to the basics of INT/EXT, Location, and DAY/NIGHT, we add the *Shot Number* and the beginning *Shot Framing*. All shots are numbered in the order that they appear in the finished edit – though, of course, they are unlikely to be taken in that order. Each is also noted with the perspective that the shot will begin. All audio is numbered to match the shot in which it appears.

The advantage of the split-column format is its perfect design for the kind of screenwriting we want to do. It forces the writer to think in terms of the final appearance on the audience's screen from the very beginning of the writing process. In other words, we can explicitly describe the finished edit in the script, instead of implying our vision. It is also better suited for short-form work, which also suits our purposes in most cases. On the other hand, scheduling and budgeting are a bit more complicated; the page-per-minute formula doesn't work here. (The run time is calculated by adding the time necessary to read the dialogue to the time of any additional action.)

If you yourself are the Producer, of course, you may choose which format (or one of the variants) to use. If you are writing for a client, they will specify which they prefer. Whichever, there is one primary question about all formats:

> Can I give my script to a Producer/Director I've never met, and have them create a production on time, on budget, and on target to my vision?

If you can say yes to that question, you are roughly halfway home. The other half of course is your vision, the unfolding of which begins in the next chapter.

5

THE SCENE DESCRIPTION

Opening the Eyes of the Audience

Who? What? Where? (Not Necessarily in That Order)

Everyone who has written short stories for fun, for profit, or for homework should quickly feel comfortable with the scene description. In content and in form, with the additional strictures of third person/present tense/active voice, the two forms have much in common. The primary difference between them – a paragraph of Scene Description contains only three elements:

Element 1 – Setting: WHERE are the people in the scene?
Element 2 – Characters: WHO are the people in the scene?
Element 3 – Action: WHAT are the people DOING in the scene?

Setting – As already discussed, the Location of each scene is specified in the Header/Slugline. As also already reviewed, the key to a good Location is to be Clear, Consistent, and Concise. Thus, the additional details of the setting make up part of the Scene Description, not the Header.

The key to good scene descriptions is The Goldilocks Principle. Once again, we are recalling our fairy tales. Ms. Goldilocks found one bowl of porridge too hot, one too cold, and one just right. In our case, we want to write setting descriptions that are not too generic and vague, not too elaborate and detailed, but just right.

Let's say you are writing a parodic commercial in which comedic ghosts sell insurance against hurricanes, featuring our heroes Jack and Jill. You could write, in the narrative format:

EXT. HOUSE – NIGHT

DOI: 10.4324/9781003410317-5

60 The Scene Description

```
JACK and JILL stop in front of a house.
```

The same thing in split-column:

VIDEO	AUDIO
1. WS - EXT. HOUSE - NIGHT JACK and JILL stop in front of a house.	1. NAT SOUND

That's not wrong, exactly, but a quick look at the variety of homes in your community will show it's also not nearly enough. On the other hand, you could write this:

```
EXT. HAUNTED HOUSE - NIGHT

JACK and JILL stop in front of a rambling, two-story greyish-
white mansion. Its faded paint is peeling; its damaged shutters
hang uselessly; its mildewed columns on the rotting front porch
tilt at dangerous angles; and of its dozen visible windows, the
few unbroken ones are filmed over with dirt and cobwebs.
```

In split-column:

VIDEO	AUDIO
1. WS - EXT. HAUNTED HOUSE - NIGHT JACK and JILL stop in front of a rambling, two-story greyish- white mansion. Its faded paint is peeling; its damaged shutters hang uselessly; its mildewed columns on the rotting front porch tilt at dangerous angles; and of its dozen visible windows, the few unbroken ones are filmed over with dirt and cobwebs.	1. SFX: WIND in the trees, CREAKING shutters, CHATTERING insects, CROAKING frogs.

Again, this is not wrong on its face – in fact, it's quite good for a short story or novel – but it is too much for the screenplay. So, like Goldilocks, we go for the description that is just right:

```
EXT. HAUNTED HOUSE - NIGHT
```

```
Jack and Jill stop in front of the Southern-style, haunted-
looking mansion.
```

Or:

VIDEO	AUDIO
1. WS - EXT. HAUNTED HOUSE - NIGHT	1. NAT SOUND
Jack and Jill stop in front of the Southern-style, haunted-looking mansion.	

Now you're probably thinking, "That's all very well, but what or who determines 'just right'?" The answer to that question is a question: *Is this detail essential for the Production Team to know to tell the story?* If the answer is yes, include it. If not, cut it.

Never forget that to create the Production, the only people who will read your screenplay are the Production Team. Your screenplay is their blueprint to build the video. It must include the information they need to construct it right, *and* it must exclude information that is not essential to the construction.

Now, the reality is that unless you yourself are the Producer/Director (and sometimes even then), the Team may take out something you put in, no matter how important you feel it to be. They may also put in something you left out, no matter how extraneous you found it. But they will always start from the script that you write.

Let's look again at our examples above. In the "too generic" example, you as the Writer, your Producer, your Director, your Production Designer, and your Location Manager are highly unlikely to envision the exact same thing when each of you read the word "house." Thus your Location Manager may find a modern log cabin, while your Production Designer is gathering furnishings for a modest split level. Meanwhile your Director envisions filming in a beachfront vacation home, and your Producer is thinking of saving money by using her own palatial estate. Getting everyone on the same page (pun fully intended) from those multiple and very varied visions is going to waste production time and production money. That waste will be blamed on you for writing a scene description so generic it ceased to be clear. Equally important, the page everyone ends on may not be what is needed to tell the story. If the Producers prevail upon the Team to shoot in their brand-new Manhattan high-rise condo – well, you could find ghosts warning against hurricanes therein, but you as a writer will have quite a task to explain it in a thirty-second commercial.

Now re-consider the "too detailed" example. In all screenplays, and especially in the short forms with which we're concerned, page space is a finite thing. In Scene Descriptions, every line that we devote to Setting is a line that we can't devote to the other two elements. Wasted detail is wasted page space. Wasted page space is wasted schedule time and wasted budget money. Said money and time will be wasted because all the detail that you will write will be almost certainly put into the picture by the Production Designer; it will be photographed by the DP; and it will be edited by the Editor. So the dominoes fall.

In my excessive detail, I just used up five precious lines describing the house where Jack and Jill stop. In all candor, I was lapsing back into novelist mode. I wanted to make the mood and tone of the setting clear, but did I have a purpose in mind for all those details? No. Now, if the detail of "a dozen visible windows" is crucial to the story, it is not an option for it to be in the scene description, it's a necessity. But I must also make it absolutely clear at some point in the script why those dozen windows are essential. The Location Manager who will have to track down a manse with exactly twelve visible windows, not to mention the Producer and the Director, will appreciate it.

That brings us to the "just right" description. If you want a location for ghosts to discuss hurricanes, "the Southern-style, haunted-looking mansion" is something the audience will probably easily accept. It is vivid enough for the Location Manager to find, or the Production Designer to create, relatively easily, while broad enough for the Team to flex their creative muscle in doing so. Just right.

Finally on settings, a word to the "applied" part of Applied Screenwriting should be said. In my part of the world, I can find a half-dozen Southern-style haunted-looking mansions, or at least houses, within a very short drive. Thus, if I am producing the screenplay myself, or if I am acting as Location Manager for the Producer who is, it's entirely practical for me to write such a Southern-style haunted-looking mansion into the script. If you are reading this in London, or Sydney, or Auckland, or Edmonton (and I'd be very pleased if you are), you probably can't. Unless you have somehow acquired a statistically improbable budget for your video, you are not traveling to where such are plentiful, either. You may not even have the advantage of a car; you may be, as once I was, a broke college student with no access to anything beyond your university and nothing to transport you but your own two legs. Do not let that discourage you. There is no shame in writing to the settings to which you have access; the thing that matters is what you do with them. That philosophy can be applied to all of what we do, including the next element.

Characters – The first time that each significant character appears in the script, they should be described sufficiently for the production team. The Goldilocks Principle applies here too: not too much detail, not too little, just enough. When we first met Jack and Jill, their narrative script read:

```
INT. JACK AND JILL COTTAGE - DAY
JACK, a sturdy, clean-cut lad, and JILL, an athletic,
adventurous young woman, smile at each other in their neat and
cheerful one-room home.

                         JACK
                   Today's the day!
```

And the split-column counterpart:

VIDEO	AUDIO
1. MLS - INT. JACK AND JILL COTTAGE - DAY	1. JACK: Today's the day!
JACK, a sturdy, clean-cut lad, and JILL, an athletic, adventurous young woman, smile at each other in their neat and cheerful one-room home.	

Notice this does not include height, weight, hair color, eye color, ethnicity, or any other specific details – because none of them are important. What is important is that the Casting Director can go out and find actors who evoke those types of characters. You are attempting to vividly communicate the kind of person that the Casting Director should seek, while giving them and the Director the creative freedom to select the individual actor who best represents their vision of those qualities. You will also note I said nothing about the clothing of the actors. I claim no special qualifications as a costumer, so I generally leave that even more in the hands of the Production Team. I trust their creativity to interpret the scene and the world of the production and costume the actors accordingly. On the other hand, if you are producing a one-person-band project – or, much more unusually, if you are a combination Writer/Costume Designer – you may choose to concisely describe the apparel of the character as well. The crucial caveat still applies; if a physical feature or a costume piece is essential to the story, it must be included.

Some fellow writers also advocate, if there is a particular actor in mind for the part, to give a brief but specific description of that individual. I advise caution in that case, however; real-world casting circumstances can render those descriptions obsolete in moments. Lastly, the initial description of the characters need only be given the first time they appear in the script. Significant changes to their original appearance must be included, but otherwise each character need only be described once.

Action – At last we have reached the central element of the Scene Description, the element where we really get to show off our chops as writers. What our people are DOING in the world that we have created for them – that's the heart of the matter, the pulse of the story, to hearken back to Chapter 2. So – how do we keep that pulse beating?

I devised a mnemonic acronym to help me keep that heartbeat steady, and to let me know when the story needs some CPR. It's called *The CAMS Credo – Concise Action Moves Story.*

Concise – I have emphasized conciseness to such a degree, I admit I could be accused of violating my own rule. Yet it is just as important here as everywhere else. Further, here we have a paradox. We are required to be succinct, and we are also required to demonstrate that we can in fact write creatively. To do that, I use three (concise) supporting principles:

1. Remember Goldilocks
2. Choose short words over long ones
3. Use a specific noun over an adjective and a generic noun, and use a specific verb over an adverb and a generic verb

To unpack that last, a bit. When I was a mere tyke, my parents gave me a little volume entitled, *Scholastic Dictionary of Synonyms, Antonyms, Homonyms*. I realize it says something about me that, at such a tender age, I was utterly taken with the book. I had already realized that similar words had different "feels." Now I had a book of similar words that proved it. Consider this entry: "bold – courageous, fearless, adventurous, brave, self-confident, forward, intrepid, dauntless, valiant, daring, audacious, lionhearted, doughty" (34). Since you have read this far in this book, I know I am preaching to the choir at this point. You can feel the connotation differences between the same denotation. Still, it's even more important in scriptwriting (to paraphrase Samuel Clemens) to use the lightning, not the lightning bug. Best of all, just as the lightning is faster than the lightning bug, the specific noun or verb is shorter than the phrases. My well-worn little book is still in arm's reach of my desk.

Action – "Actions speak louder than words." "What you do speaks so loud I can't hear what you say." "You can talk the talk, but can you walk the walk?" Clichés? Perhaps – but only because they're true. In screenwriting, they are especially true. **What your Characters do ultimately reveals who they are.**

Your Production Team is reading your script to create the final product. The final product must reach the final Audience, and another name for the Audience, of course, is the Viewers. Viewers may quote memorable lines, but they believe memorable action. I say this as one who loves great dialogue, who will quote it at any appropriate moment and some inappropriate ones. In short-form work especially, it's not enough. Have your Characters DO something in character, and that something must lead to the next point.

Moves – Each scene in our screenplays should lead to the next scene; each shot within the scene should lead to the next shot. Moving pictures should move. The engine that can drive that movement is this: ***If you insert a new Header for a new scene, at least one of your Characters must be in a new place.*** Remember, a new Header means cast, crew, and all must pack up, move to a different place or time or both, set up again, and start shooting. That much effort must be justified, and what justifies it is the Character herself or himself being in a new place.

By "new place," I do not only mean physical place. I mean that something happens in the current scene that moves your Character to a new place intellectually or emotionally – ideally both. The Character thus has a reason to be in the new place physically, thus justifying the new Header, thus moving the story forward. As we will discuss in the next chapter, the same principle should be applied to shots as well. All is in service of the final point...

Story – Everything leads back to Story. I'll not rehash previous chapters here, but I do want to emphasize a point. In the kind of production we are primarily discussing, the Story must also advance the Client's message. If Jack and Jill's adventures in the haunted manse prompt no interest in hurricane insurance, the script is ultimately a failure, no matter how entertaining the commercial spot might be. This is equally true if you are your own client, and you are trying to persuade the Audience of your own message. No matter how passionately you believe in your own cause, if the Audience is left unpersuaded, it is not a good script, even if it was a good story.

Learning to weave story and message together is, candidly, one of the toughest parts of Applied Screenwriting. The analogy from Chapter 2 – "Get your Protagonist up a Tree, throw rocks at them, get them down one way or another" – can be useful in thinking about this process. What need or want that your Message addresses might send your Protagonist up a tree? What opposition to your Message is throwing rocks? What product or service (including the Public Service of the PSA) of your Message will get your Protagonist down happily? Organically including the answers to all, or even one, of these questions may help integrate message and story. However, there are some items that, tempting as they might be, must NOT be included. Or at least, must not be included in the wrong way.

Who, Where, and What to Leave Out – Or Not

Backstory as Character Memory – Detailed character histories can be excellent preparation for creating strong Characters, regardless of the length of your project. As I mentioned in Chapter 2, though, they should never be shared in their full glory in Act I. It is a case-by-case decision whether any of your characters' backstories need to be shared at all. *Back* story, after all, essentially states that the story is "back" in the past. However, whether or not you decide to put the backstory in the script, it must never be in the scene description as a character's memory.

An example of what NOT to do with this case:

```
INT. JACK AND JILL COTTAGE - DAY
JACK, a sturdy, clean-cut lad, and JILL, an athletic,
adventurous young woman, smile at each other in their neat
and cheerful one-room home. Jack thinks back fondly to the
night he proposed to Jill, remembering the starry sky, the
```

blue dress Jill wore, and the promise he made to her then to
bring water from the hilltop into the cottage he will build
for them.

The problem here is that there is no way for the Audience to see and hear Jack's memory. Now, if it is important that the Audience experiences that memory, it must be written as any other scene – only with the included information that it happens in the past of the story:

```
INT. JACK AND JILL COTTAGE - DAY
JACK, a sturdy, clean-cut lad, and JILL, an athletic,
adventurous young woman, smile at each other in their neat and
cheerful one-room home.
EXT. TOWN SQUARE - DAY
Title Over:
                    Two Years Earlier
In the tiny but picturesque center of their village, Jack
kneels in front of Jill. The engagement ring in his hand
sparkles in the sunlight.
                         JACK
               I'll build us a home, I'll bring
               water from the hill straight into
               it - Jill, will you marry me?
Jill bursts into joyous tears.
```

Now the audience will see what Jack is remembering so fondly. In split-column, it might look like this:

VIDEO	AUDIO
1. MLS - INT. JACK AND JILL COTTAGE - DAY	1. NAT SOUND
JACK, a sturdy, clean-cut lad, and JILL, an athletic, adventurous young woman, smile at each other in their neat and cheerful one-room home.	
2. MS - EXT. TOWN SQUARE - DAY	2. JACK: I'll build us a home, I'll bring water from the hill straight into it -
In the tiny but picturesque center of their village, JACK kneels in front of JILL.	
CG: Two Years Earlier	

VIDEO	AUDIO
3. CU - EXT. TOWN SQUARE - DAY The engagement ring in his hand sparkles in the sunlight.	3. JACK: - Jill, will you marry me?
4. CU - EXT. TOWN SQUARE - DAY JILL bursts into joyous tears.	4. NAT SOUND

Thoughts and Feelings – If memories cannot be experienced by the Audience unless the Screenwriter writes them as scenes, even more invisible are the Character's thoughts and feelings. Portraying the emotions is of course the province of the Actors. But even the best thespian in the world can do nothing with a scene description in any format that reads:

```
INT. VILLAGE BAKERY - DAY
Jill is in line to pay for her fresh bread, as the plump,
prim homemaker in front of her stares indecisively at the
other baked goods. Jill thinks to herself how much she
wishes the woman would just make up her mind. Jill's got a
full agenda for the day and this isn't helping her keep it.
As the woman continues to dither, Jill thinks of all the
other things she could be doing at this moment. With each
new thought, Jill gets a bit more annoyed.
```

Again, though, if it's important that the audience hear Jill's thoughts – without sharing them to her baker and her fellow shopper – it can be done. In this case, the best solution is a simple voice-over:

```
INT. VILLAGE BAKERY - DAY
Jill is in line to pay for her fresh bread, as the plump,
prim homemaker in front of her stares indecisively at the
other baked goods.

                    JILL (V.O.)
            Would you please make up your mind?
            I've got a lot to do today!
```

This is virtually identical in split-column:

VIDEO	AUDIO
1. MLS - INT. VILLAGE BAKERY - DAY Jill is in line to pay for her fresh bread, as the plump, prim homemaker in front of her stares indecisively at the other baked goods.	1. JILL (V.O.): Would you please make up your mind? I've got a lot to do today!

Dialogue – Writing conversation into the description is a tricky point. In other words, is it permissible to simply write "Characters X and Y talk" without scripting each line of dialogue? The short answer is – it depends. The general principle is, if conversation is done by background actors as part of the sound ambiance of the scene, it need not be scripted out. If the conversation is from an Actor with other scripted lines, or if the conversation introduces a point to the Story, write it out. Back to the bakery:

```
INT. VILLAGE BAKERY - DAY
Jill pays MR. STONE, as the hum of conversation from several
other shoppers fills the store.

                    JILL
          Thanks so much Mr. Stone - I'd
          love to stay and chat, but I'm
          in a terrible hurry!

                    MR. STONE
          Of course, Jill - have a nice day!
```

What exactly the other shoppers say isn't important; that their talk creates the impression of a thriving business is. That Jill is in a hurry is important, though – another case-by-case distinction, but one that is clear and consistent.

Anything the Audience Cannot See or Hear – This is the bottom line of the description. If an Actor can't act it, a Production Designer can't find or make it, or a Sound Designer can't create it, it doesn't go in a Scene Description. To finally determine what does go in, ask yourself the Primary Question of scene descriptions:

> Can my Production Team use my script to make the Audience see what they need to see to get the message?

That will determine if your Audience needs to see it or hear it. *How* they need to see it is the subject of the next chapter.

Works Cited

Scholastic Book Services. *Scholastic Dictionary of Synonyms Antonyms Homonyms*. Scholastic Book Services, 1972.

6
CAMERA AND LIGHTING
Focusing the Eyes of the Audience

You've just crossed over into . . . the SCREEN-writing Zone.

Beginning this chapter with this paraphrase from one of my favorite classic American TV series should raise your eyebrows. "OK, man, if we're just crossing over into screenwriting, what have you been writing about all this time?" you might rightfully ask. Certainly, I have been writing about screenwriting, and so far, I have been focusing mostly on the parts of storytelling that we share with other and more venerable media. As mentioned earlier, storytelling principles go back to the earliest oral traditions. Stories organized into discrete scenes that tell their tales through acting, visuals, and sound are the essence of theater. Now, though, we are taking a step even beyond that.

As anyone who's ever seen a well-done stage play will testify, sets and lighting can do wonders in focusing an audience's attention, but they have their limits. When my daughter was a child, she appeared in her first youth musical production. . . . In the chorus. When she came on, the leads were downstage, acting their little hearts out (and quite well for their age, I hasten to add). The production designer and the Director had done an excellent job setting the stage so that I would watch the stars act, too. Yet my attention was focused on the back row of the ensemble. That's where my daughter was, and I focused there *because I could.*

Add a camera to the mix, though, and I might not have been able to focus on my daughter. The shot might be only of the two primary actors singing to each other, or of one only, or even of only the eyes of one actor. That is the first of the wondrous elements of our field. *The camera is the eyes of the Audience; they see exactly and only what the camera shoots, and how it shoots it.*

DOI: 10.4324/9781003410317-6

Here lies one of our greatest challenges, or paradoxes, as we work with Production Teams, as described in Chapter 3. Creating the look of the shot, its lensing and lighting, is the responsibility of the DP and the Camera Department, under the leadership of the Director. As with Actors and their performances, DPs are quite protective of their turf, as they should be. Our responsibility as writers who are part of the team is to make our vision as clear as possible to the DP and the Director, while never even suggesting that our vision trumps theirs. On the other hand, if we are also the Producer/Director for the production, we will be making those production decisions ourselves; writing that vision as specifically as possible will make executing them much easier. At the same time, we must recognize that the circumstances of the production almost certainly will force changes to the script. In both cases, our screenplays will not be clearer than our understanding of camera and lighting and their effect on the final screen experience.

Lighting and Color – The Defaults Are Your Friends

As previously noted, and as shown in Figure 6.1, visitors to the set will usually be astonished at the number of lights and the complexity of the setups that are needed just to make the scene look natural.

In a nutshell, this is because our brains and eyes work together at a capacity far beyond the most sophisticated camera. Today, I drove in through

FIGURE 6.1 The DP Works above the Cast; Just Some of the Light Fixtures Needed for the Effect Are Visible.

brilliant sunshine to my office building; I entered and walked down a hall lit by fluorescent lights; from there I entered my office, where I turned on an incandescent bulb. I unconsciously adapted to three very different lighting scenarios. To get the same natural effect with even the top pro cameras, such that the audience never notices the transitions from one kind of light to the other, would take hours of work from expert crews. In fact, professional camera crew members estimate that most of the production day is devoted to lighting. If you are already in production at an entry level, an emphasis on good lighting is one of the fastest paths to professional respect.

If you are solely the writer, though, good lighting is something that can be as unstated by you as it is unnoticed by the audience. In most US and UK productions, *naturalistic lighting* is the norm, the "default mode," illustrated in Figure 6.2.

When you write the scene descriptions, if you make no mention of any special lighting needs, the Camera Department will light to express the time and setting of the scene. You need only note the exceptions. Of course, those exceptions to the rule can be mightily effective, but full discussion of all such is a text of its own.

One such variation is near and dear to my heart, though. It is also easy to see in a still photo. Best of all, it is easy to set up, even for a one-person crew. That is the famous "Universal Horror" lighting effect. I grew up watching all

FIGURE 6.2   The Antagonist Shown in a Shot Taken by the DP While on the Ladder Shown in the Previous Photo (Figure 6.1).

the Universal Studios horror movies on late-night television: Dracula and his Daughter, Doctor Frankenstein and his Monster and his Monster's Bride, and all the rest of the classic creatures. Later I would learn that the creators of these movies borrowed heavily from German Expressionism – in fact, some of the creators were original German Expressionists. Even as a kid who'd never heard of expressionism, German or any other nationality, I noticed that these venerable, thrilling movies just looked different from anything else I saw on TV. One of the techniques that made that difference was simply lighting the subject from below, rather than from above. The reversal of the everyday light is enough to make even a good-looking and friendly talent look foreboding if not terrifying, as in Figure 6.3.

It helps that this illustration, like the frightening features from Universal, is in monochrome – "black and white." That was the default for almost all the output of Hollywood's studios in the Golden Age. In moving picture production today, at all levels, color is the default and need not be specified in the screenplay. Monochrome, or monochrome with one exception in the frame (such as the famous shot of the little girl in the red coat from Spielberg's *Schindler's List*), should be written; if the whole production is in monochrome, you need only say so at the beginning.

Camerawork – The Defaults May Not Be Your Friend

So much seems straightforward, especially in the Applied Screenwriting projects which are our focus. As I stated earlier, the camera is the eyes of the Audience. Most of the viewers in that audience are used to seeing things in living color and illuminated from above. In short, audiences expect natural color and lighting. I find it a relief that we don't have to specify it on each page of the script.

Camerawork also has defaults. Absent further direction, crews will use these as well. Unlike color and lighting, though, default camerawork is unlikely to produce the creative results desired because the default for the camera is not the default of the eye. When we look at anything – a person, a place, an object – we do not stare rigidly at our subject from a fixed position. What we look at may not change; how we look at it changes as often as we blink. In human vision, this process is largely an unconscious one. In camerawork, it should be a carefully considered sequence because each choice of angle affects how the audience literally sees the subject. In music, playing the note right is as important as playing the right note. In moving images, shooting the subject right is as important as shooting the right subject. As with music, playing or shooting right is much easier when we begin by writing right. And just as the two staffs of music are the treble and the bass, there are several primary concepts for camerawork in storytelling.

Camera and Lighting **73**

FIGURE 6.3 The Antagonist, Lit in the "Universal Horror" Style.

Key Concept 1: Camera Height or Level Relative to Subject Affects the Audience's Perception of the Subject

When most of us shoot our first videos, we often hold the camera at our eye level. If we use a tripod, we put the camera at a height where we can comfortably look into the viewfinder. In other words, we set up the camera on our own eye level. Sadly, some videographers – even some who call themselves professionals – never advance much beyond this approach. Neither do many writers.

For both screenwriter and shooter, this is a mistake. We can see the mistake when we consider some common expressions. When we say we "see eye to eye" with someone else, we are saying we agree with that person, and that that agreement is between equals. When we emphasize that we are telling someone else the truth, we say that we are "on the level" – again, between equals. On the other hand, if we say that we "look up to" someone, we are saying that we consider them superior to ourselves in some respect. If we say someone "looks down on" someone else – well, most of us rarely admit we do that, but we know it means whoever we said it about thinks the third person is inferior to themselves.

Or think back to your childhood. We literally look up to the adults around us; our physical position reflects the power imbalance that they have over us. Now that we ourselves are grown, the opposite is true again; physically, we look down at children. For this reason, anyone who works with kids will tell you that a key step to connecting with them is getting down on their eye level.

These expressions and perspectives play out exactly in the camera. If the camera is on the subject's *Eye Level*, the audience and the subject are literally seeing "eye to eye." The audience will perceive the subject as an equal to itself. The audience will also infer that the subject is neither more nor less powerful than the world in which they find themselves.

Consider Figure 6.4. The photographer has used the ***rule of thirds*** – basically, dividing the screen up like a tic-tac-toe board and using the intersection of the lines to compose the shot – to place the eyes of the subject, in this case our Antagonist, at exactly the point that our eyes naturally look. No power advantage or disadvantage is implied; in fact, the implication is that the audience should identify with the Antagonist at this point. To achieve this effect, the photographer adjusted himself to the shot, instead of the other way round.

If the camera is placed below the subject's eye level and shoots up at the subject, a *Low Angle*, the audience is looking up to the subject. The subject will appear more powerful, possibly more threatening, to the audience. The audience will expect that subject to deal with their setting more effectively as well. Figure 6.5 illustrates this concept.

Given that the table limits how low the camera can go, notice how much more ominous our Antagonist appears with so much more of the background above him visible. This illustrates the adjustments the photographer made based on the practical situation.

Camera and Lighting **75**

FIGURE 6.4 The Antagonist Subject Shot at the Antagonist's Eye Level.

FIGURE 6.5 The Antagonist Subject Shot at a Low Angle, beneath the Antagonist's Eye Level.

The opposite in eye levels is also true. If the camera is placed above the subject's eye level and shoots down at the subject, a *High Angle*, the audience is looking down on the subject. The subject will appear more vulnerable to the audience. The audience will expect that subject to deal with their setting less effectively. As shown in Figure 6.6, even our Antagonist seems lessened by the view from almost directly above him. (This is why Antagonists are rarely shot this way; we want our audience to see them as more powerful, not less!)

This raises another important point: subtle differences in camera angle can be as effective as extreme changes. Returning to our earlier point about likability, a Protagonist facing off against the Antagonist for the first time might be shot at a slight High Angle to place them in the role of the underdog. The same character would probably be shot at Eye Level when conversing with their best friend, as would the friend themselves. Finally, in their moment of triumph, the Protagonist might be shot at a slight Low Angle to emphasize their victory. In all three cases, the point is to render the character more relatable, more likable, to the Audience.

In sum, the position of the camera relative to the shooter's eye says nothing; the position relative to the subject's eye says a great deal. The audience may not be able to articulate the differences between subtle height variations such as those shown above, but they will read those changes into their understanding of the production.

This same principle applies, incidentally, whatever the subject of the videography. The most important thing in the shot is always the subject. Usually that's a person, but it may be an inanimate object. Most objects don't have eyes, but they do have a usual height from which most people perceive them. Moving the camera above or below that level produces the same effect.

"That's fine for the DP," you may be thinking, "but how do I communicate that as a writer?" Here's where we begin to ask ourselves not only what we see but how we see it. Look back at the illustrations in Figures 6.4, 6.5, and 6.6, and think how you might describe them.

Here's my take:

```
INT. CARD ROOM - DAY

We see the GAMBLER gaze over the table, a chip held in his
hand.

We see the GAMBLER loom large over the table, a chip held in
his hand.

We see the GAMBLER shrink away from the table, a chip held
in his hand.
```

FIGURE 6.6 The Antagonist Subject Shot at a High Angle, above the Antagonist's Eye Level.

To repeat, these may seem very small, almost insignificant differences. Candidly, I agree. If you are handing your script off to a buyer, all you can do is imply how you see it. The Director and the DP can and will do what they want. On the other hand, if you are creating the project yourself, and you wish to get specific – that's the province of the split-column. It might look like this:

```
VIDEO                                          AUDIO

1. MS - INT. CARD ROOM - DAY                   1. SILENCE
At EYE LEVEL, we see the GAMBLER gaze
over the table, a chip held in his hand.

2. MS - INT. CARD ROOM - DAY                   2. SILENCE
We see the GAMBLER loom large over the
table, a chip held in his hand.

DISSOLVE TO:
3. MS - INT. CARD ROOM - DAY                   3. SILENCE
We see the GAMBLER shrink away from the
table, a chip held in his hand.
```

The initials "MS" at the beginning of the header designate the initial framing of the shot. This brings us to the second key:

Key Concept 2: Camera Distance from Subject Affects the Audience's Perception of the Subject

In human relationships, physical distance and emotional distance are bound together. The closer we are to another person emotionally, the more comfortable we are with physical closeness. Obviously, the closer we are to another person, the more detail we can see in their face – or whatever part at which we might be gazing – and that detail furthers the closeness.

Since the camera is the eyes of the audience, the same principle applies in moving images. The closer the camera is to the subject, the closer the audience is, both physically and emotionally. Conversely, moving the camera back literally distances the audience from the subject. In fact, it might almost be said that moving the camera back far enough changes the subject – the most important thing in the shot – altogether, such as from the Characters to the Setting.

The point to keep in mind: as you are sitting at your word processor, imagining the final product, you visualize not only what happens but how the camera frames it. All you need do is describe what you're seeing. In the split-column format, you do so with the frame abbreviations in the header. The standard abbreviations, their meanings, and their illustrations are:

1. *eXtreme Long Shot/eXtreme Wide Shot (XLS/XWS):* The two terms "Wide" and "Long" are used interchangeably to denote a panorama at or near the broadest possible perspective on the scene. Which you choose is mostly up to you, unless you are working with a Director or Client who has a preference. Figure 6.7 shows the ultimate effect of this type of shot. The Characters therein are barely visible, overwhelmed by the landscape – which itself is not particularly overwhelming, but the perspective makes it so.
2. *Long Shot/Wide Shot (LS/WS):* Also a broad perspective, the LS/WS moves the balance of the shot from the Setting toward the Characters, though the Setting is still predominant. The LS/WS is often used as the *establishing shot*, the initial shot that shows where everything in the scene is located in relation to each other. Figure 6.8 shows the difference; the background is still prominent, but we are close enough to our Characters to see faces and expressions – in short, to begin to establish individuality.
3. *Full Shot (FS):* The FS captures the human subject from just above the top of the head to the soles of the feet. With this perspective, the emphasis has shifted from the Setting to the Character. As in Figure 6.9, the landscape has become background; the frame is dominated by the people in it. This is also a good example of the *two-shot*, two Characters holding the frame and the Audience's attention.

Camera and Lighting 79

FIGURE 6.7 An Extreme Wide Shot/Extreme Long Shot (XWS/XLS) of Our Protagonists in an Urban Park.

FIGURE 6.8 A Wide Shot/Long Shot (WS/LS) of Our Protagonists in an Urban Park.

FIGURE 6.9 A Full Shot of Our Protagonists in an Urban Park.

4. *Medium Long Shot/Medium Wide Shot (MLS/MWS):* Also known as the three-quarters (¾) shot, this shows the person from the knees to the crown of the head. A somewhat dated variation of this tightens the shot slightly, from roughly mid-thigh to the top of the hat the subject is wearing. I specify "hat" because this shot originated in American Westerns; it was designed to show the "good guy" from the top of his white Stetson to the tip of his six-shooter's holster, and thus became known as the "cowboy" shot. As Figure 6.10 shows, we are now close enough that one Character can hold the shot on their own.
5. *Medium Shot (MS):* The Character is shown from the waist up. This is the closest shot that balances the audience's attention on the character, while keeping a sense of emotional objectivity. Once again, as shown in Figure 6.11, one Character fits comfortably in this type of shot; placing two Characters in this or even the three-quarters shot implies a stronger connection between them.
6. *Medium Close-Up (MCU):* Also known as the Bust Shot, this frames a person from mid-chest and shoulders up. Figure 6.12 shows the individual dominates the frame in this type of shot; we have moved beyond usual social distance to the beginning of intimacy with the Character.

Camera and Lighting **81**

FIGURE 6.10 A Medium Long Shot/Medium Wide Shot (MLS/MWS) of One of Our Protagonists in an Urban Park.

FIGURE 6.11 A MS of One of Our Protagonists in an Urban Park.

82 Camera and Lighting

FIGURE 6.12 A Medium Close-Up (MCU) of One of Our Protagonists in a Studio.

7. *Close-Up (CU):* The frame shows only the Character's face. As you can see in Figure 6.13, this is a truly intimate framing; every nuance of expression will be captured by the camera. A variation of the CU is even more intimate:
    Figure 6.14 shows a standard modification of a CU is called the "Choker"; just below the mouth to just above the eyebrows, it is even more emotionally intense.
8. *eXtreme Close-Up (XCU):* The camera is focused on one detail of the Character's face. "The eyes are the mirrors of the soul," goes the old saying, and this shot usually focuses on the eyes, as in Figure 6.15. It can, of course, have other parts of the Character as its subject, depending on circumstances.

Several framing variations may be used and scripted along with any of these camera-to-subject-distance choices. One is the ***Dutch angle*** or ***Dutch tilt***. Like the "Universal Lighting" scenario, Dutch tilts were a hallmark of German Expressionism – the "Dutch" is a corruption of *Deutsch*, the German word for "German." In all the previous illustrations, you will have noticed that the frame of the picture seems level with the ground or floor. In the Dutch tilt, as shown in Figure 6.16, the camera is deliberately tilted so that the frame is not perpendicular to the walls and parallel to the floor. This conveys a sense of emotional or psychological imbalance, as the picture itself is imbalanced.

A second is the ***Over-the-Shoulder (OTS)*** shot. As the name describes and Figure 6.17 shows, the primary subject (facing the camera) is shot over the

Camera and Lighting **83**

FIGURE 6.13 A CU of One of Our Protagonists in a Studio.

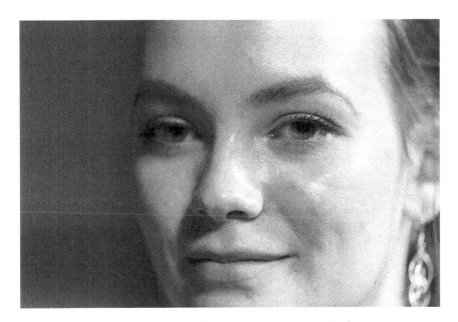

FIGURE 6.14 A "Choker" of One of Our Protagonists in a Studio.

84 Camera and Lighting

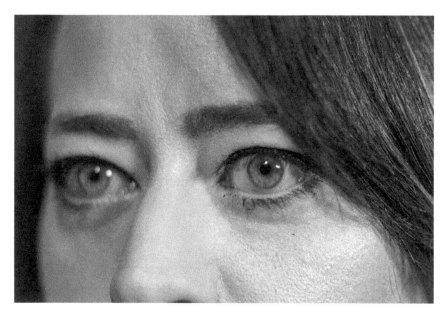

FIGURE 6.15 An Extreme Close-Up (XCU) of One of Our Protagonists in a Studio.

FIGURE 6.16 A Dutch Angle/Dutch Tilt of the Antagonist.

FIGURE 6.17 A Shot of One of Our Protagonists from Over-the-Shoulder of the Antagonist at the Card Table.

shoulder of the secondary subject. This shot is foundational to most conversations between two characters, as it focuses on the speaker (usually) while keeping the relationship between the two in the shot.

A third is the *Point-of-View (POV)* shot. In this setup, the camera view duplicates what the eyes of a character in the scene would see. It is often, though not always, accompanied by some kind of framing device to show that the character in question is looking through something. For example, the standard sequence of submarine movies where the captain looks into the periscope, followed immediately by a shot of an unsuspecting ship in the center of a circle of crosshairs. In Figure 6.18, the Director is framing a shot through his hands as the Producer looks on impatiently. The next shot, Figure 6.19, shows what our intrepid auteur sees through his hand-made viewfinder.

It bears emphasis that the Audience will have been placed in the Director's shoes for the shot. Temporarily, they will be a character in the scene, and therefore the clearer we can make such POV shots (as with the hand trick), the better.

Since people are the foundation of the Story, all terms and examples are defined in terms of human beings. For good or ill, though, in commercial and corporate work, a product may be the true "star" of the production. Fortunately, these terms can be easily adapted to inanimate objects. For example, the Low Angle shot of a "mountain" of chips (Figure 6.20) was created by

86 Camera and Lighting

FIGURE 6.18 A Two-Shot of Producer and Director as the Latter Frames the Shot.

FIGURE 6.19 The Chips on the Table, Framed by the Director.

FIGURE 6.20   A Low Angle of a Stack of Chips Gives a Heroic Perspective to an Inanimate Object.

moving the chips close enough to the edge of the table to be able to place the camera below the chips themselves.

Similarly, a Full Shot of a car would be bumper-to-bumper, while an XCU might be a headlight. Keep in mind an XCU of a headlight is going to have a similar effect as an XCU of a person's eyes. The Audience probably will not feel the same emotional connection with an automobile as with a human being, but it will feel an equivalent interest in the detail being shown. The top priority, when you use framing terms to describe how you see the shot of the inanimate object, is to be consistent. If an XCU of a car is a headlight, a CU is the front grill, a MCU is the hood area, an MS includes the windshield, and so on, those terms should always describe approximately the same area of the car; that is, if the XCU of the front of the car is one headlight, the XCU of the rear is one taillight. It should go without saying that camera-to-subject distance for a demonstration video is determined by the demands of the process. A needlepoint video might be shot almost entirely in CUs and XCUs, while a martial arts demonstration might never come closer than the MS.

What does not go without saying is the difference between moving the camera to a new framing and zooming the camera to the same perspective. As you may be aware, "*zoom*" means changing the focal length of the lens, without moving the camera itself. A "zoom in" increases and a "zoom out"

88 Camera and Lighting

decreases the magnification, the size in the frame, of the subject. What many people fail to realize is that changing the focal length of the lens changes more than the size of the subject. To illustrate, Figures 6.21, 6.22, and 6.23 are all CUs of one of our Characters seated in exactly the same place on the set.

The first, Figure 6.21, was taken with the camera zoomed out all the way – that is, with the smallest focal length possible. The camera was then moved toward the subject to achieve the CU framing. Notice that our Character's face appears relatively flattened; also notice that the background is completely out of focus.

The second, Figure 6.22, used a focal length approximating normal human vision (said focal length varying between cameras), and the camera was backed up from its first position to get the proper frame. As you see, the face appears much more natural, and we can see some details in the background.

The third, Figure 6.23, was taken with the camera zoomed in all the way – the largest focal length – and placed the furthest from the subject to maintain the CU. Now our Character's face appears unnaturally elongated, and we see quite a bit of the background.

For those of us who are shooting our own productions, the point should be obvious; achieving a pleasing CU of a Character is not just a matter of zooming in and out to achieve a CU. For all of us, the point is more subtle; scripting a zoomed-in CU will produce a different effect than scripting a

FIGURE 6.21 A CU of the Antagonist, Shot by Zooming the Lens Out and Moving the Camera In.

Camera and Lighting **89**

FIGURE 6.22   A CU of the Antagonist, Shot with a "Normal" Focal Length Zoom and Adjusting Camera Distance Accordingly.

FIGURE 6.23   A CU of the Antagonist, Shot by Zooming the Lens in and Moving the Camera Out.

natural one. Zooms, and their effect on the image, are also a part of our third key:

Key Concept 3: A Moving Camera Shot Must Be MOTIVATED

In split-column work, the default is a static shot – the camera doesn't move while the shot is being taken – and, thus, does not have to be scripted. As you imagine your completed production, though, there will be times when you see the perspective of the shot changing. In other words, the camera moves.

The movement that you see in your head falls into one of several types. If you see the camera turning left to right or vice versa while otherwise staying in one spot, like turning your head, that's a *pan*. If you see the camera inclining up or down while otherwise staying in one spot, like nodding your head, that's a *tilt*. If you see the camera moving closer to or further away from the subject, that's a *dolly*. And if you see the camera moving parallel to or with the subject, that's a *truck*.

Probably, the most common camera move isn't really movement at all; the aforementioned on-camera *zoom*, where the videographer changes the focal length during the shot. Candidly, people with a features or dramatic series background abhor zooms. The rest of the video world accepts them within limits – because they are so cheap and easy to do, they are usually overdone.

On the other hand, another "non-movement," the *rack focus*, is not so often seen in non-cinematic work. In a rack focus, the operator adjusts the *depth of field* during the shot. The depth of field is simply the area on the line from the front of the lens to infinity that is in focus during the shot. Most features and dramatic series use shallow depth of field; relatively little in front of or behind the subject is in sharp detail, and the foreground and background is in soft focus. In fact, shallow depth of field is usually the first thing meant when someone discusses "the cinematic look" of a production. You can see this in Figure 6.24.

The Character closest to the camera is in very soft focus, while the one seated further away is clear and sharp, and the background behind her is in soft focus again.

In contrast, most of the rest of production – especially corporate and social media work – uses deep depth of field; as shown in Figure 6.25, virtually everything from the camera to the farthest horizon is in focus.

Little more needs to be said about the radical difference between the two otherwise identical shots. Except this, with the reliance on deep depth-of-field, rack focuses are rarely seen in most independent and inexpensive video work. Properly done, though, they can change audience perspective as effectively as a zoom, without the stigma attached to the latter. Figures 6.26 and 6.27 show this. One is designed to make the Audience concentrate on the

Camera and Lighting 91

FIGURE 6.24 Our Two Protagonists Seated on an Urban Park Bench in a Shot with Very Shallow Depth of Field.

FIGURE 6.25 Our Two Protagonists Seated on an Urban Park Bench in a Shot with Very Deep Depth of Field.

92 Camera and Lighting

FIGURE 6.26 A Perspective on the Table Shot with the Cards in the Center of a Very Shallow Depth of Field.

FIGURE 6.27 A Perspective on the Table Shot with the Chips in the Center of a Very Shallow Depth of Field.

Camera and Lighting **93**

hand of the Antagonist; the other is designed to make the Audience focus on the growing stakes of the game.

Generally, this is the limit of the writer's vision, even in split-column work. If you are the Producer/Director, you may even go a step further and designate the mechanism with which to do the shot. We introduced the specialties in Chapter 3; each has a different effect on the image, though, and thus the audience perception. *Hand-held* movements use only the shooter to perform them, as shown in Figure 6.28.

This can create a dynamic camera movement. Given the limitations of human physiology, though, any movement will be unavoidably shaky, no matter how experienced the Cinematographer. Since journalists and documentarians are often forced by time constraints to work handheld, this type of movement is closely associated with news and cinema verité production.

The *Tripod* mount is much more stable and is the most common means of camera support; as Figure 6.29 shows, though, it also limits your movement to pans and tilts, unless you also acquire a *dolly* to move the whole assembly through space.

Camera stabilizer mounts, aka Steadicam®, combine the fluidity of the tripod with the freedom of hand-held operation. They allow for incredibly smooth hand-held shots while the operator moves along with the subject, as the operator is preparing to do in Figure 6.30.

FIGURE 6.28 The Cinematographer in a Classic "News Shooter" Hand-Held Stance.

94 Camera and Lighting

FIGURE 6.29   A Director/Cinematographer and His Crew Behind-the-Scenes of a Short Subject Movie.

Finally, *drones* literally make the sky the limit in terms of camera movements. In the behind-the-scenes illustration, Figure 6.31, the cinematographer has just launched the drone.

The resulting shot, Figure 6.32, is a *bird's eye view* of the scene from more than a hundred feet up, offers a perspective that, in this extreme long shot composition, is quite as distancing though far more breathtaking than the horizontal Extreme Wide/Long Shot perspective.

Whichever you choose, though, the key concept remains: *all movement must be motivated.* There must be a reason for each time you, as a writer, instruct the Production Team that the camera moves during the shot. There are three reasons for my emphasis on this axiom: one practical, one aesthetic, and one storytelling.

The practical reason for motivated camera moves: camera movement inflates your budget. This is obviously crucial in our focus on independent work. If you want a move requiring equipment, you have two options: (1) buy the gear and learn to operate it yourself; (2) rent the gear and hire an operator. Fortunately, neither of these choices is as expensive, for any gear, as it once was. Unfortunately, any additional cost is an additional cost. Further: let's say you already own a fluid-head tripod and are quite comfortable executing a smooth pan with it. This is probably the simplest move/equipment

Camera and Lighting **95**

FIGURE 6.30   The Cinematographer Wearing the Camera on Its Stabilizer Mount as His Crew Assists Its Setup.

FIGURE 6.31 The Cinematographer with Drone in Action.

FIGURE 6.32 The Drone's Final Perspective of Our Two Protagonists and the Urban Park.

combo. Murphy's Law, though, applies in production like nowhere else; anything that can go wrong will, and a camera move is one more thing that can go wrong. Things going wrong adds takes; more takes add time; and time, of course, is money. First and foremost, the use of camera movement is literally a cost-benefit analysis.

The aesthetic reason for motivated camera moves is a bit more subtle. As we will discuss, the rules of editing have changed from the era of silent features to the social media market. Even so, audiences still expect that a shot will start with the camera stationary, and that the camera will come to rest again before moving on to the next shot. As a result, a shot with a five second movement should take up at least five seconds of screen time. Time is precious in video, and for any of a host of reasons, you may need to shorten that time. If you cut away from that shot during the movement, the edit will be noticeable and distracting to the audience. To put it in other words, is the time necessary for the movement worth the time it takes in the finished product?

The storytelling reason for motivated camera moves is related to the aesthetic reason. *Camera movement says what's at the beginning of the shot is important, what's at the end of the shot is important, and what's in-between is also important.* I repeat: especially in short-form work, onscreen time is precious, and camera movements require time. If you spend that time, everything from beginning to end of the move should be important to the story.

For example, Jack and Jill are sitting at opposite ends of a row of desks in college. (It's a flashback to before their marriage.) Good old Professor Curmudgeon is addressing Jack and Jill's class, announcing a new scholarship. If, as the professor speaks, we see a CU of Jack and then one of Jill, the audience sees the scholarship will impact either or both. If the camera begins on Jack, then as the professor speaks trucks down the row, past Jack, Karen, Lee, Maria, Nina, Oscar, and Pat, finally coming to rest on Jill, the audience will assume all eight students relate to the scholarship – and that the coming production will show how they relate. The relation among shot elements brings us to the fourth key:

Key Concept 4: "Shooting for the Cut" Starts with Writing for the Edit

As we will see in the next chapter, all our shots must be brought together in what used to be called the cutting room. (Today it's the room in which the computer editing platform is housed.) As you may have gathered, I am all about specificity. Still, some ideas relating to both cinematography and editing should guide your screenplay without being written there. The questions below need not be answered in your headers and shot descriptions; answering them as you write, however, will make your project easier to both shoot and cut.

1. *What should be the Establishing Shot?* Most scenes begin with, and virtually all scenes contain, the shot that shows where everything is in relation to each other. When used at the beginning, the shot also establishes the environment, the time, and the mood of the scene.
2. *Should I use a Master Shot?* The master shot is the entire scene, from beginning to end, in one shot. Many Directors will call for one in the

process of shooting the scene. There is a difference between shooting a master shot that will become part of a finished whole, though, and shooting a master shot that is the finished whole. As a rule, I avoid the latter in favor of the next two questions:

3. *What are important (or at least useful) Cut-Ins and Cutaways?* A Cut-In is a CU of a significant object in the scene. For example, in the story of our card game, all the CUs of the hands could be used as Cut-Ins. When scripted, they serve to emphasize important parts of the scene – contrasting one player's strong hand with another's weak one. A Cutaway is a shot of a significant object not in the scene but related to it; for instance, a CU of the world-famous (and public domain) "Welcome to Las Vegas" sign would be a useful Cutaway. It gives us some clue to where our game is taking place; at the same time, the sign is obviously not in the card room, and is probably not essential to the story. Detailing Cutaways in the script saves time trying to think of them on the set and gives your editor (you) more options. I freely admit, when producing my own scripts, I seek out as many Cut-Ins and Cutaways as possible, especially unscripted ones. Like love, a timely Cut-In or Cutaway covers a multitude of sins, at least of the continuity variety.

4. *What are important Reaction Shots?* A shot of a Character reacting to an action or line of dialogue may do as much to tell the story as the action or dialogue itself.

    If we cut to the photo of our Protagonist immediately after a hand is dealt, as in Figure 6.33, the expression on her face sends a clear message about her hand to the Audience. Of course, it also sends the same clear message to her opponents at the poker table. Which raises an interesting point; is she acting for the table, even more than the Audience? Only the showdown would tell for sure.

5. *What are important Two-Shots?* As noted earlier, a two-shot is simply a shot of two characters together in the frame. The choice of who is framed together, and when, may also go a long way toward advancing the story. An example is Figure 6.18, the two-shot leading into the POV; with that visual, dialogue between the Producer and the Director almost seems superfluous.

This brings us back to the challenge from the beginning of the chapter. If you are the Producer/Director as well as the screenwriter, you can write your script with the assurance that you will produce it to the camera specifications you described – or at least you'll have the chance to try. If not, all the production choices will be out of your hands. You can only imply the production you see in your mind's eye. That being the case, I recommend that split-column be used for the former, and screenplay format for the latter. (In Appendix 2,

Camera and Lighting **99**

FIGURE 6.33 Our Protagonist Reacting to Her Cards.

I provide examples of the differences between the cinematographic implications of narrative and the camerawork specifications of split-column for the same scene.) I also recommend, as an exercise to develop your abilities in this area, to choose several of the example photos from this chapter and describe them as clearly but concisely as you can, in a narrative screenplay. However, as you write, do not use any of the camera terms or abbreviations, and do not provide readily identifying features of the actors or costumes. Then, share the descriptions with some friends, asking them to select the described shot. The more your readers get right, the more you know you're on track.

Whether you are writing for yourself as a one-person-band, or you are selling your screenplay to a production company, the primary question is the same: *"Can my Production Team use my script to make the Audience see what I want them to see the way I want them to see it?"* If so, you can begin to consider the question of *when* the Audience needs to see. That is the subject of the next chapter.

7
EDITING

Moving the Eyes of the Audience

Putting It All Together ... as the Clock Ticks Relentlessly On

Rock & Roll Hall of Fame musician Bob Seger, in his 1980 hit, "Against the Wind," wrote and sang "Deadlines and commitments, what to leave in, what to leave out." It's become my favorite description of editing. Once the Camera crew has done their work, and all the shots of Characters, Setting, and Action have been completed, when and how the Audience is shown those shots is the responsibility of the Editor. If each shot is a glance into the world of the Story, the Editor assembles them all into a coherent vision of the whole. Since the Editor is also the last person on the Production Team to work on the project, theirs is also the world of the final deadline and ultimate commitment.

As I have noted more than once, Producers, Directors, Production Designers, Directors of Photography, Cast – all may make choices that not only do not match our conception but also may counter it. Even if we ourselves are Producer/Director/"Star"/and so forth, the real world in which we work may force changes to what we have written. The same thing is true, to an extent, in the cutting room. Ralph Rosenblum, whose editing credits include *Annie Hall* and *The Producers*, freely admitted in his memoir *When the Shooting Stops* that his documentary background left him "generally feeling comfortable taking liberties with a script" (92). He also quoted Oscar ™ nominated screenwriter and Director Philip Dunne as saying, "A film editor is also in effect a writer" (99). Fellow editor Walter Murch, who cut *Apocalypse Now* and *Ghost*, among others, essentially agrees, saying in *In the Blink of an Eye* that the editing process is "not so much a putting together as it is a discovery of a path" (4).

DOI: 10.4324/9781003410317-7

On the other hand, even in the world of big-budget features, editors acknowledge from whence the footage with which they work sprang. Rosenblum also emphatically states, "(F)or a film to be good, *everything* [emphasis in original] has to be good" (135). He also acknowledges *Annie Hall* specifically as a case of finding the heart of the original shooting script (290). Murch again assents, saying the script guides the first look at the production footage and essentially opens the creativity of the editor (47).

This is especially true in the school of editing which dominates US and UK production, *continuity or "invisible" editing*. As the nickname states, the goal of continuity editing is to make the transition between one shot and the next as unobtrusive as possible. Rosenblum flatly says, "No viewer should walk out of the film saying, 'I really dug the editing'" (2). Viewers should think that they are watching the action unfold naturally, from the best viewing point for that moment in the story. Murch unfolds a fascinating theory, expanding on a thought from Golden Age writer/Director John Huston, that this type of editing reflects the human action of blinking, which in fact inspired his title (59–63). Without going too far into the technical details, though, Murch, Rosenblum, and all other continuity editors agree: the Audience should never notice that their perspective on the scene has been changed for them by the choice of the editor. In short, the Editor seeks to immerse the Audience in the story that we have written.

Non-continuity or discontinuity editing, on the other hand, is in all ways the opposite of invisible. This style seeks either to make the transitions between shots as obvious as possible or to disregard visual continuity altogether in favor of some other element that holds the piece together. The music video which assembles striking but unrelated shots to the beat of the music is perhaps the most familiar of these. A premiere example of this is the justly famous video of Queen and David Bowie's collaboration, *Under Pressure*. All of the musicians involved were at the height of their careers; thus, they had such hectic schedules that none of them had time to act in a video separately, let alone together. Faced with this unpleasant reality, creators David Mallett and Andy Morahan edited together silent film classics and industrial stock footage to make the music video. The unforgettable result evokes the song and the bands to this day – despite not a single frame of Bowie, Freddie Mercury, Brian May, Roger Taylor, or John Deacon. Somewhat less memorably, documentaries and corporate videos in which a narrator's voice-over connects images with no other relationship between them follow the same discontinuity principles. Both these genres are common in the short-form market; neither aspires to the kind of storytelling we have discussed; and yet, both connect at least as strongly back to the original script.

Some say that the *montage* theory is a halfway house between continuity and discontinuity. Briefly, montage is the concept that the juxtaposition of two shots may create a meaning that is different from and greater than either shot alone. Montage has been thoroughly developed by Russian filmmaker and film theorist Sergei Eisenstein, based on the work of his predecessor Lev Kuleshov. Kuleshov's groundbreaking experiment in montage was amusingly illustrated by Alfred Hitchcock in his discussion with Francois Truffaut of *Rear Window*:

> In the same way, let's take a close-up of [actor James] Stewart looking out of the window at a little dog that's being lowered in a basket. Back to Stewart, who has a kindly smile. But if in the place of the little dog you show a half-naked girl exercising in front of her open window, and you go back to a smiling Stewart again, this time he's seen as a dirty old man!
> *(Truffaut 216)*

Whichever approach the Editor chooses, they will be most influenced in their choice by the screenplay we have written. As the previous chapter implied, the more clearly we can envision how a project is shot, the more clearly we will envision how it might be edited. Even if another editor takes the project down another path, they will appreciate clarity, if only because they themselves have so many choices to make.

How many choices might that be? The formula that determines how many different ways shots can be combined in one scene was published by Murch, again in his text *In the Blink of an Eye* (79–81). The formula is

$$C = (e \times n!) - 1$$

C equals the minimum number of ways a scene can be edited. n is the total of all shots taken. E is the mathematical constant that is the base of all natural logarithms, approximately equal to 2.71828. The exclamation point is not for an interjection; in this case, ! indicates the factorial function, in which one multiplies all positive integers up to and including the number itself.

That's a lot of math for a screenwriting book. Here is a basic example. We shoot a conversation between Jack and Jill with one master-wide two-shot, one MS OTS of Jack from Jill's perspective, one MS OTS of Jill from Jack's perspective, one CU of Jack, and one CU of Jill – five shots total. For this scene, so common in the real world, the equation would be: $C = (2.71828 \times 5 \times 4 \times 3 \times 2 \times 1) - 1$; $C = 325.1936$; **three-hundred and twenty-five** ways to edit one simple scene of five shots. And, to drive the point home, such a scene is at least as likely to be found in a corporate short video as a premium series or tentpole feature.

That being the case, some concept of how to narrow the hundreds or thousands of edit choices is essential. Once again, we come back to the script itself. As we write, those choices will become clearer as we understand two vital creative elements of editing: ***rhythm*** and ***tempo***. Both are nearly identical to the musical concepts. Rhythm is the regularity of the time between edits, the "beat" of the cuts. A production in which all the shots are roughly the same length – that is, one in which the times between edits are roughly equal – will be perceived as very rhythmic. A project in which each shot has a different duration than the ones before and after it will be perceived as more arrhythmic or even chaotic. Tempo, also called pace, is the length of time each shot is onscreen, the amount of time between edits. The greater the number of edits in a given time, the "shorter" the shots will seem, and the faster the tempo. Fewer edits in the same amount of time creates the opposite effect, slowing the pace and making the shots seem "long." (In Appendix 2, I provide examples of the differences between the implications of narrative and the specifications of split-column for editing the same scene.)

Both rhythm and tempo may be affected by the choice of *transition* between shots, as well. Editing replaces one onscreen image with another; how it does so is the transition. In modern editing, there are five basic kinds of transitions. The oldest transition, going back to the earliest days of cinema, is the *cut*. One shot ends, the next one begins. The cut is the "default" transition for all forms of moving images; in both narrative screenplay and split-column, the Editor will always cut first absent input from script or Director. It is also the instant transition in terms of real time; the interval between one frame and another is faster than human perception. That makes it the fastest transition in terms of editing tempo. It also makes it the so-called invisible transition; in other words, if your goal is continuity editing, the cut is usually the least noticeable.

The other four types of transition all have this in common; in their editing effects, they are the opposite of the cut in every way. All other transitions are visible; they are designed to be noticed. All other transitions are not instant; they require a certain amount of time to take place, though the precise duration is chosen by the Editor. Finally, all other transitions are not defaults; using them is a deliberate creative choice.

Of these transitions, the dissolve and the fade are probably the oldest (historians are undecided which came first). Fades may be "In" or "out." In a *fade-in*, the video begins with a black screen; the shot gradually becomes brighter and brighter until it replaces the black screen altogether. A *fade-out* is the opposite; the shot begins at full brightness and gets dimmer until full black is reached. A *dissolve* is a simultaneous fade-out of one shot and fade-in of the next. Of the time transitions, these are the least obtrusive and therefore the most common, though still a distant second behind cuts.

Like the dissolve and the fade, the wipe and the iris are similar in concept and effect. In a *wipe*, one shot at full brightness replaces the other, also at full brightness, as a border between them moves across the screen. The wipe can move in any direction: top to bottom or vice-versa, left to right or the opposite, or from any corner. An *iris* is similar, except that the second shot begins as a pinpoint and expands as a shape within the first one – usually a square or circle, though any shape may be chosen by the Editor. The various *Star Wars* movies provide plentiful examples of these in action.

Finally, the computer age introduced the ***digital effect.*** One shot replaces the other with virtually any shape, pattern, or motion you can imagine. A very common example is the "page turn" or "peel," in which one shot seems to be peeled off the next like turning a page in a book. They can be quite visually striking, but consequently they are the most obtrusive of the transitions.

As with the rhythm and tempo of the edit, the transitions convey information to the viewer as well. More than a century of moving images taught the Audience "rules" of transitional meaning. A cut between one shot and the next was the transition between one instant of time and the next. The dissolve, the wipe and the iris signified a change in place or time or both. A fade-out followed by a fade-in signified a clean break between one story and what followed; it is often still used in television to begin and end commercial breaks.

Speaking of advertising: as far as digital effects are concerned, when I was starting out in the profession they were often called "used car effects." They signified very little, but because they are so attention-getting digital effects were often used to add visual pizzazz to otherwise at-or-below-average budget productions – like local used-car commercials. This stigma has faded a bit; still, like ghost pepper hot sauce, a little digital effect goes a very long way.

Just as the digital stigma has faded, so the conventions above have moved to conventions from their Golden Age status of solid rules. If you choose to break any of them in your script, you may. Recognize, though, that doing so will automatically call the viewer's attention to the edit, not the project's message. Once you have changed the information of the transition, be consistent in the transition's use. In other words, if you choose to write a page turn to signify a change in place and time, every page turn should do so. (On an immediate practice note, virtually all presentation software packages, such as PowerPoint, include most of these effects. Just create two slides and you can change the transitions between them to your heart's content, to fully absorb the effect of each.)

This brings us back to the fourth key concept of the previous chapter, which is the key concept of this one:

"Shooting for the cut" starts with writing for the edit.

To emphasize a point made earlier, the split-column script is designed for edit and shot specificity. If you are asked to provide a split-column script to a Production Team, and the Team shoots exactly to your script, the Editor should be able to assemble the footage with only your screenplay for guidance. If you are the Team, you'll be following your own instructions to the end.

The narrative screenplay format, in contrast, allows a bit more specificity for the writer concerning the edit, but not much. Basically, within scenes you can specify nothing; between scenes, you can specify any transition you want. Let's check back in on Jack and Jill's progress for an example:

```
INT. JACK AND JILL COTTAGE - DAY
JACK, a sturdy, clean-cut lad, and JILL, an athletic,
adventurous young woman, smile at each other in their neat and
cheerful one-room home.
                    JACK
          Today's the day!
                    JILL
          (kisses Jack)
          I can't wait!
They shoulder their backpacks; Jack gallantly opens the door
for Jill, and she precedes him outside.

EXT. VILLAGE-TO-HILL ROAD - DAY

Jill and Jack step out of their small yard onto the path that
leads to the hill in the distance. With another exchanged smile,
they stride off into the rising sun.

                    DISSOLVE TO:

EXT. HILL ROAD - AFTERNOON

Jill and Jack plod along the steepening path.

                    JILL
          This is interesting.
```

In split-column, it would look like this:

VIDEO	AUDIO
1. MLS - INT. JACK AND JILL COTTAGE - DAY	1. JACK: Today's the day!
JACK, a sturdy, clean-cut lad, and JILL, an athletic, adventurous young woman, smile at each other in their neat and cheerful one-room home.	

2. MCU - INT. JACK AND JILL COTTAGE - DAY JILL kisses JACK.	2. JILL: I can't wait!
3. MS - INT. JACK AND JILL COTTAGE - DAY They shoulder their backpacks; Jack gallantly opens the door for Jill, and she precedes him outside.	3. MUSIC: folk instrumental.
4. WS - EXT. VILLAGE-TO-HILL ROAD - DAY Jill and Jack step out of their small yard onto the path that leads to the hill in the distance. With another exchanged smile, they stride off into the rising sun. DISSOLVE TO:	4. MUSIC: folk instrumental CONTINUES.
5. MS - EXT. HILL ROAD - AFTERNOON Jill and Jack plod along the steepening path.	5. JILL: This is interesting.

Finally, the Primary Question of editing expands on the primary questions of Descriptions and Camera: "*Can my Production Team use my script to make the Audience see what I want them to see the way I want them to see it, and when and how long I want them to see it?*" You will notice that, so far, all our primary questions have specified "*see*." You may be wondering, since we rarely work in silent film anymore, when we will discuss what the audience *hears*. Naturally, that is the subject of our next chapter.

Works Cited

Murch, Walter. *In the Blink of an Eye*. 2nd ed., Silman-James Press, 2001.
Rosenblum, Ralph, and Robert Karen. *When the Shooting Stops*. The Viking Press, 1979.
Truffaut, Francois. *Hitchcock*. Simon & Schuster Paperbacks, 1984.

8
AUDIO

The Ears of the Audience

> Before I was your age, television was called radio.

This very loose paraphrase of the Grandfather in William Goldman and Rob Reiner's motion picture, *The Princess Bride*, is a very strict statement of fact. During the "Golden Age of Radio," listeners in the United States and the United Kingdom were as numerous and as loyal to the same genres of programs that populate television, then and now. In the very earliest days of TV, not only the genres but many of the shows were direct transplants from radio. Some, like the police procedural *Dragnet*, the Western *Gunsmoke*, and the soap opera *The Guiding Light*, lasted decades longer than their radio originals. It is small wonder that television was often thought of as radio with pictures added. This emphasis on the audio side continues to a certain extent in American broadcast and cable television to this day. Most of us have had the TV on in the background while we did something else; despite not having focused on the screen, we ended the program with a fairly clear idea of what happened.

"If that's so," you may be asking, "why have we spent so many chapters on the visuals, and only now one chapter on audio?" Fair question. First answer: the ascension of streaming is changing the audio-first approach. The hits that have leapt from Netflix and the other streaming services to become household words demand a focus on the image that is unprecedented, in English-language television at least. I am beginning to see a "trickle-down" effect from these shows to the other video media; it is well to write for that, even though our focus is not on the streaming series.

Second answer: the corporate, commercial, education, and training markets – almost all client-based short-form video, in other words – have

DOI: 10.4324/9781003410317-8

been even more audio-swamped than high-end television. If early television was radio with pictures, applied video has been slide shows with narration. Bluntly, audiences are sick of it. In a world awash in video, the fastest way to make your projects stand out is to give them something that actually needs to be watched. This is especially essential in training work, where you are showing your viewer how something should be done.

And yet . . . here is the paradox. Image is essential, and audio is also essential. All research shows audiences will stick with a piece that has technically bad visuals and good audio much longer than they will a project with technically good visuals and bad audio. If you've ever tried to "watch" a program in which the audio is static ridden, distorted, and harsh, you can attest to this yourself. If you produce your own projects, the application is obvious. Since the audience insists on hearing our project clearly, it is important that we as writers give the sound designer audio worth hearing. Toward that end, let's discuss the five elements of audio.

Element 1: Dialogue (and Parentheticals)

What your characters say and how they say it can be unforgettable, even in, or especially in, short-form work. The commercial catchphrases of yesterday and today would probably make a book on their own. But how do you write dialogue that has that kind of impact?

I'm afraid I have no certified, sure-fire, long-term-warranty formula for that. If I did and deigned to share it, you'd be paying considerably more for this tome. I can, however, recommend six things that will do much to improving your dialogue, no matter where you feel you are in the craft right now.

Step 1: Before You Write, Listen to Real People

On the one hand, a good writer should be a good listener. Rhythm and tempo are as important to dialogue as they are to music or to editing. The more you really concentrate on what other people are saying, the more you will absorb these paradoxically obvious and intangible sensations. On the other hand, a good writer must be a selective listener. Try this experiment, next time you're out with friends. Ask if you can record some of the conversation. Then do so. When you play it back, ignore the first few minutes of the recording. Awareness of the recording will completely kill the naturalness of the conversation. Once your friends have forgotten about it, and that should be fairly quickly, you will easily hear the change. Transcribe a few minutes after that point. Odds are, what you read will be . . . just awful. In real life, people don't finish their sentences; they cut each other off; they talk over each other; they use single words that mean volumes to others in the group, but nothing to those outside. In short, they write lousy dialogue. Dialogue is not conversation; it is the illusion of conversation. This leads to the next step:

Step 2: Before You Write, Listen to Great Characters From the Genre You're Writing

I am not suggesting that you plagiarize anyone. I am saying that if, for example, you want to write a film noir parody for your promo video, listen to the dialogue in great noir pictures. The slang tossed around by hard-boiled gumshoes as they pack heat through the gin joints of their world is part of this, of course. As your ear develops, you'll notice that the rhythm and tempo of dialogue in this genre, and in all others, are just as distinct. I believe this should be a matter of concentration because being influenced by the existing media is unavoidable. If you are consciously analyzing your own influences, you are less likely to unconsciously copy them, and you are far more likely to produce work worthy of them. (In Appendix 3, I recommend a list of features that are, in my humble but professional opinion, worth studying purely for their dialogue and, as one reviews them, worth concentrating on the voices unique to each Character and the rhythm and tempo unique to each movie.)

Step 3: Before and as You Write, Listen to Your Characters

All characters are people, individuals. All individuals have voices as unique as they are. As you have conceived the people whose drama you are recounting, you should have begun to hear their voices. Not, one hopes, literally, but you already know that your Protagonist and your Antagonist would do something as simple as inviting others into their respective homes in very different manners. You as their writer know what they need to say; they, even though a part of you, know how they might say it.

Step 4: As You Write, Script the Best Synthesis of the Above

The message of your project, the illusion of real conversation, the poetry of screen dialogue, and the voices of your characters can come together to create, for lack of a better term, magic. Once again, there is both the challenge and the reassurance: working in short-form, micro-budget video, whether client commissioned or social media channeled, does not affect this principle. The same actor could read the lines of our old insurance friends Jake and Doug, and you'd not mistake one for the other. Even two characters from the same insurance company world, like Jamie and "Doctor" Rick, speak distinctly.

The most important thing you can add to your talent to get these distinct voices is time. As far as is in your power, give yourself the time to let your character's talk echo in your imagination. Then take more time to do two more steps already mentioned:

Step 5: After You Write, Read It Aloud

Briefly, if you can't read it, neither can anyone else – but just because you can, doesn't necessarily mean anyone else can. So, finally:

Step 6: After You Write, Have It Read Aloud

In much of the world, virtually every town of any size has a community theatre scene. Get involved; make friends; then ask those friends to do a table read. Listen to them read. Take notes. Discuss with them afterward. Finally, work in what works.

Speaking of what works, and what does not, raises the question of parentheticals. The technical details of parentheticals were discussed at length in Chapter 4. What we now consider is not the what of their use but the when and the if.

Voice-Overs – In narrative work, voice-overs are most often used to hear a character's inner monologue. It was a staple of American crime thrillers of the 1940s and was revived in some of the "neo-noirs" that followed. A few works outside the noir genre use an outside narrator's voice; for example, the Grandfather with whom we began our chapter is reading the book *The Princess Bride* to his grandson, and occasionally his and the boy's voices are heard over the fictional adventures of Westley, Buttercup, Inigo et al.

Note the word "occasionally" in the last sentence. Voice-over is very much like hot sauce; a little goes a considerable way in narrative productions. If you find that a solid minority of your dialogue is your Protagonist voicing her thoughts, it is probably a good idea to backtrack your script. Either provide a character to whom she can speak her thoughts or – even better – figure out a way that her actions will show what she is thinking.

The voice-over is also the heart and soul of the "slide show with narration" approach to corporate, commercial, education, and training video. Its overuse has marred even more lavishly funded documentary series and features. As I said earlier, audiences are sick of it. Full disclosure, though: I have worked on more than one project where the client insisted on using their employees as the on-camera talent. These were good people and skilled workers, more-or-less comfortable doing their jobs on camera, but they were not actors and never wanted to be. In other words, the voice-over became a necessity. It wasn't until I had been in the field for quite a while that I hit on a solution.

Make the Voice-Over a Dialogue, Instead of a Monologue

Just having two voices on the soundtrack instead of one goes a long way toward retaining audience interest. It also allows a bit of character development for your two narrators, such as a new hire questioning an experienced employee about the process shown on screen. Finally, two voice talents instead of one are unlikely to impact your budget significantly, which makes this an attractive real-world approach to a real-world issue.

Off-Screen – The difference between Voice-Over dialogue and Off-Screen dialogue is the line's place in the fictional world. A Voice-Over is heard only by the audience and, possibly, the character "thinking" it. It is not audible in the scene itself, and no other characters react to it. An Off-Screen line is said by someone who does not appear in the shot but is physically present in the scene. It is audible, and onscreen characters can and usually do react to it. Unlike the Voice-Over, though, off-screen lines have not become conventions or clichés of any genre. They tend to arise naturally in the script. Keep in mind that Off-Screen dialogue pulls the attention of both the characters and the audience *off-screen*, though. If what is going on in the shot is where you want your audience focused, that's not a good time for someone out of the shot to speak out.

Languages and Media – The short rule is, if your production needs a line in another language or sounding as if it came from an electronic medium, feel free to insert the appropriate parenthetical. Unless your audience is entirely bilingual, it's a good idea to subtitle any additional languages. In the scene description, simply note, "The [second language] lines are subtitled in [primary language]," and you're good to go.

Bits and Delivery – Parentheticals for bits and delivery should be the rarest element in any screenplay that you write. There should literally (in the true sense of that word) be no way for the Director and the Actor to figure out the desired action and intonation on their own. The overuse of the parenthetical in this manner is a universal red flag to the people who buy narrative screenplays, which is why I am emphasizing the point again.

"But I'm writing for myself," you may be thinking. "Why shouldn't I use as many parentheticals for bits and delivery as I want?" Good question. If you are writing for yourself and you are following my recommendation, you are using the split-column format. That being the case, visible actions are written in the Video column. Bits are visible actions. Q.E.D. Delivery is audio information, of course, but if you're directing your own work, parentheticals for delivery are extraneous. You as the Director should be able to remember and communicate the delivery you want to your own Actors.

That said, there are times when you may choose to write and direct the narrative screenplay format. Even if you are one-person-banding it, aim for the professional standard. The effort to conceive your descriptions and dialogue clearly without resorting to parenthetical bits and delivery will only improve all your screenplays in the long run.

ADR: A Note for the Producing Writer

Despite your Production Team's best efforts, there will be times when even the best lines get lost in production. Usually that happens because the video was both elaborate and perfectly executed, but for whatever reason the audio was not. Rather than spend the time and money to take it from the top, the Director will say those allegedly magic words, "We'll fix it in post," and begin planning for an **ADR** session.

ADR is short for Automated Dialogue Replacement, also known in the UK as post-synchronization or post-sync. In its simplest form, the talent watches the video and delivers their lines again as an audio engineer records the speech. From a writer's point of view, this is something we cannot and do not wish to script for. But if you are producing your own work, it is an option to keep in mind. As a graduate student helping out another thesis project, I once had to build a makeshift ADR booth in a dorm room using soundproof blankets and C-stands. Still, with the able and willing talent that we had, even that got astonishing results. And, though we don't write for it, ADR does come back to the writer with one solid principle: *never throw away your script until the finished production is out to its audience.*

Element 2: Music

Music is the oldest element of sound for moving pictures. From virtually the beginning of so-called silent pictures, movies were accompanied by music. The cheapest and smallest independent nickelodeons had a hard-working pianist tickling the ivories at a tinny piano. The studio-owned downtown movie palaces had enormous pipe organs with virtuoso organists. For premieres and special engagements, they might even have full orchestras. The days of live musical accompaniment for features are long gone, of course, but the importance of music and its subjective effect on the audience remains undisputed.

What is disputed is the relationship between the music and the mood of the production. *National Lampoon's Animal House* is a case in point. Producer Ivan Reitman and Director John Landis agreed that the score for the picture should be serious in nature, a counterpoint to the over-the-top hijinks on screen. To that end, they engaged famed dramatic composer Elmer Bernstein. He wrote exactly the kind of stirring, solemn music desired, and the rest is history (Simmons 110–111). Yet none of these artists had any quantifiable guarantee that the approach would work. Of all elements of our productions, music is perhaps the ultimate subjective.

That said, I want to focus on the major objective points about music. The first is the difference between *diegetic* and *non-diegetic* music. Diegetic sound is sound that exists within the scene; it is most often used in reference to music, though it includes dialogue and sound effects as well. To continue the *Animal House* references, Otis Day and the Knights' now famous Delta House performance of "Shout" is diegetic music. In short form, the countless commercials in which the cast spontaneously bursts into the products jingle are all diegetic as well. Non-diegetic sound does not exist in the scene but is still heard by the audience; scores such as Mr. Bernstein's and the various kinds of voice-over are non-diegetic.

Whether you choose diegetic or non-diegetic music is entirely your creative choice. If you choose diegetic, make it clear in the scene description from whence the music issues – a jukebox, a car radio, a live band, whatever. It's important to note here that music and all other audio components are allowed much greater specificity in the narrative screenplay than the camera and editing elements. You may script any and all music that your imagination hears in your scene . . . within one practical limit.

That limit is the second objective point of music: ***Music in production requires copyright permission.*** In fact, under US copyright law, it requires two basic permissions of *copyright licenses.* The first is the permission to use the composition, the musical notation and lyrics (if any) that make up the song. The second is the permission for the recording, including all the artists involved. This is simply to include the music in your soundtrack. Depending on the media in which you intend to distribute your production, you may need up to five separate additional licenses. If this sounds complicated, it is. It is also expensive. I am not a lawyer, nor do I play one on TV, so I will leave it at that – except to say that buying the vinyl, CD, mp3 or any other recording of a song *does not* give you the right to use it in your production. If you want to use any music that you did not write, play, and record yourself, you have two options. Option 1: do the research, hire the professionals who specialize in obtaining rights, and pay the money to license the song. Option 2: use only *public domain* music.

Public domain works are creative materials that are not protected by copyright law. Most commonly, the copyright has expired, or the material has been deliberately placed outside copyright protection by the creator. Both types are thus available for general use without payment, though some require screen credit in the resulting productions. The digital age has brought archives of public domain music within a browser search of independent Producers. This in turn makes it easy for writers to preview the tunes and bring them into their creative process. If you know you cannot afford the rights to your favorite band's best hit song, you will be much better off imagining the music that you can use as part of your project from the early stages.

Element 3: Sound Effects (SFX)

Any noise that is neither music nor dialogue but which must happen at a certain point in the script and to which characters should react is a ***sound effect*** (abbreviated *SFX*). As with music, all SFX may be specified in the script, in the scene description for narrative screenplay, and in the Audio column for split-column scripts. A particularly creative use of SFX, both aesthetically and financially, is to create the illusion of an event that is too dangerous and/or expensive to actually produce; for example, the sound of a car crash on the soundtrack, while the visuals are Characters "seeing" and reacting to the accident. Beyond this, the world has a practically limitless supply of sounds, any of which may be essential to the story. Use as necessary, but keep in mind, all noises are not SFX.

Element 4: Ambient/Background/"Nat" (Natural) Sound

Noises that are not SFX, but which are common to the setting, are called, variously, ambient sound, background sound, or natural "*nat" sound*. From a writer's point of view, the only time nat sound need be mentioned in the script is when it is the only sound on the audio track. From a production point of view, as you may have already discovered, the problem is not usually getting nat sound; the problem is keeping unwanted nat sound out.

Foley: Another Note for the Producing Writer

Wanted nat sound, on the other hand, may be equally challenging. Furthermore, needed sound effects are not always recorded on set. In both cases, even with the enormous digitally available sound libraries of today, we screenwriters will be relying on the talents of the *Foley artist*. These talented individuals create "nat" sound that sounds truly natural, and sound effects that affect the Audience. My personal favorite of their work is that done in the "Foley pits." These are squares filling the floor of the recording studio, each just big enough to walk in place, composed of every imaginable material on which human beings walk. A rack on the wall of the studio is also filled, in this case with everything imaginable in which human beings walk. The Foley artist watches the raw video with three things in mind: the surface on which the actor is walking, the shoes the actor is wearing, and the rhythm of the actor's steps on screen. Then the Foley artist puts on the correct shoes, steps in the correct box, and walks at the correct rhythm as the sound of their steps are recorded. Granted that this may be beyond low-budget costs, which may bring us to the last audio element. . .

Element 5: Silence

The rarest thing on the soundtrack is absolute silence. This is not the same thing as a scene with no dialogue, music, or SFX but with recorded sound; that's a nat sound scene. This is no recorded audio at all on the soundtrack. In narrative terms, it might be used to simulate the point of view, or "point of hearing," of a Character who is unable to hear. Outside that very specific use, it is basically a way to immediately catch the audience's attention because of its rarity. Because of its infrequent use, and to distinguish it from nat sound, it must be scripted as with music and SFX.

Audio Transitions and Terms

As with editing visuals, transitions may be used between audio elements. There are three basic transitions in audio, and one which combines audio and visual elements. The *cut* is the same effect as with video; one sound begins and ends at full volume. The second, the *fade*, also has the same effect as its visual counterpart. In a *fade-in*, the audio begins at zero volume and increases gradually to full strength; the *fade-out* is the opposite. A variant of each is the *fade-down* and *fade-up*, in which the sound goes from its current level to a lesser or greater volume. This is often accompanied by designating one sound *under*, meaning at a lesser volume than another. The third, the *crossfade* or *segue*, is the audio equivalent of a dissolve; one sound fades out as the next fades in. Finally, a *split edit*, also called a **J-cut** or **L-cut**, is a manipulation of a video and an audio cut. In the J-cut, the audio from a second shot begins before the end of the first shot; in other words, the Audience hears shot 2 before it sees it. An L-cut is the opposite; the audio from the first shot continues past the cut to the second shot – the Audience hears shot 1 after it has begun to see shot 2. In the graphics of editing software, they look something like this:

Shot 1 Video (L-cut)	Shot 2 Video	Shot 2 Video	Shot 2 Video	Shot 3 Video (J-cut)
Shot 1 Audio (L-cut)	Shot 1 Audio (L-cut)	Shot 2 Audio	Shot 3 Audio (J-cut)	Shot 3 Audio (J-cut)

Again, all may be specified in the script in the Audio side of the split-column or in the scene descriptions of the narrative. An L-cut in the latter would begin to describe the next scene's audio at the end of the previous scene; a J-cut would begin the description of the next scene with the last audio from the previous one.

This brings us to the Primary Question of audio. Once again, it expands on the primary questions of Editing, Descriptions, and Camera: "*Can my Production Team use my script to make the Audience see* and hear *what I want them to see* and hear *the way I want them to see* and hear *it, and when and how long I want them to see* and hear *it?*" If all those can be answered in the affirmative, your script – and you – is ready for the final chapter.

Works Cited

Simmons, Matty. *Fat, Drunk and Stupid; The Inside Story Behind the Making of Animal House*. St. Martins Griffin, 2012.

9

THE CONCLUSION

The Effect on the Audience

> Welcome back, fellow mermaids and mermen. We've learned to make our H_2O. Are we ready to swim in it?

We have spent the previous eight chapters with one goal in mind: visualizing the produced video as fully as possible, then communicating our vision in script form, which will become the produced video. Now, we hope, we are ready to do it "for real."

That is, as ready as we can be. At this writing, "Artificial Intelligence" has burst into the industry with all the force and even less predictability than an EF 5 tornado or a magnitude 9 earthquake. Humility regarding my own prophetic powers, plus the desire to keep this volume from being outdated before it goes to press, keeps me from saying much more. Except this, the moving image industry has been dealing with disruptive new technology at least since *The Jazz Singer*. We will adapt to AI too. The only question is how.

Answering that question, or beginning to, I believe the words of wisdom of Coverdale and Marsden (of the classic rock group Whitesnake) still apply. "I don't know where I'm going, but I sure know where I've been," began their 1982 hit song. Therefore, as promised in Chapter 2, listed below, in no particular order, are a handful of the texts (available from this publisher) that I have found helpful and inspirational in my own work, and which branch out from the highway I've traveled in this book:

- Edward Fink, *Dramatic Story Structure: A Primer for Screenwriters*. This book is exactly what it says on the cover – an in-depth exploration of the narrative foundation beneath the script. The structure in question is

DOI: 10.4324/9781003410317-9

the oldest in Western literature; Fink relates Aristotle's *Poetics* to modern mass media in ways both surprising and inspiring.
- Edward Dmytryk, *On Screen Writing*. It is perhaps the most methodical approach to screenwriting from a cinema veteran, whose four-decade career stretched from the Golden Age to the Hollywood New Wave. His other books on acting, directing, editing, and cinema in general are equally worthwhile.
- Ken Dancyger, Jessie Keyt, and Jeff Rush, *Alternative Scriptwriting: Contemporary Storytelling for the Screen*. Some might consider this the opposite of the previous two works. However, it is not that the authors reject structure; they reject formula and in the book give a solid approach to using the first without falling into the other.
- Matt Stevens and Claudia Hunter Johnson, *Script Partners: How to Succeed at Co-Writing for Film & TV*. Writing is generally considered a solitary pursuit. This book is a solid explanation of how to approach it as a collaborative endeavor while keeping your collaborator as a friend (or at least staying on speaking terms).
- Thomas Crowell, *The Pocket Lawyer for Filmmakers; A Legal Toolkit for Independent Producers*. As I said earlier, I am not a lawyer, nor do I play one on TV. (I did play one in community theater once, but that's neither here nor there.) Still, I would be remiss if I did not recommend this text to anyone who tackles this business as an entrepreneur. While independent feature work is an important part of the text, most is equally applicable to all video or media work.

Equally applicable is Lasswell's communication model. A quick review, fully applied to Applied Screenwriting, looks like this:

- *Who*: You and the Client, or You AS the Client
- *Says What*: The Video Production *Founded on* The Script
- *In Which Channel*: Moving Images with Synchronized Sound
- *To Whom*: The Audience *Through* the Production Team
- *With What Effect*: The Effect as Conceived in the Script

From this, we must distill two essential points.

First point: if we are doing work for hire for a Client, we are communicating for them. We have asked the first, two-part, Primary Question, "Who's the boss, and what do they want?" After sufficient time, we have answered both parts in detail. In the answering process, we have also answered the second Primary Question, "Why should I care?" In fact, we have answered it on two levels: why the intended Audience should care, and why the Client should care. The latter may take some explanation and friendly persuasion on our part, but we must answer it.

Second point: if we are sending work for hire to a Production Team, we are communicating through them. More than one screenwriter has compared sending off the finished screenplay to sending a child off to school. That may seem melodramatic. The analogy does apply, though, in that it is now out of your hands. The Producer, the Director, the rest of the Production Team, and the Cast will now ask the same ultimate Primary Question that you did from their perspective: "*Can we, the Production Team, use this script to make the Audience see* and hear *what we want them to see* and hear *the way we want them to see* and hear *it, and when and how long we want them to see* and hear *it?*" Yes, the "I" has become "We," and the "We" may not come up with the same answers as the "I."

One more time, we writers get good news and bad news – and some more good news. The good news: it is rare, though not unheard of, that a commissioned script is completely junked. The bad news: it is even rarer that a screenplay is produced precisely as written. The further good news: hard as it may be for some of us to admit, change is not always bad. The reason that *most* people *become* professionals in any of the specialties in our business, as in most other fields, is because they love and are good at the work. The reason that *all* people *remain* professionals in any of the specialties in our business, as in most other fields, is because they love and are good at the work. In other words, the smart Applied Screenwriters welcome the input of the fellow professionals, whose job is to make their work look and sound as good as it possibly can.

Ultimately, working with Clients and Teams is not unlike being a residential architect: listening to homebuilders describe their dream home, creating the best blueprint possible of that dream house, and then giving the contractor and constructors the blueprint, trusting them to interpret it, all the while believing that the homebuilder will be happy with the result. Your responsibility ends with the "blueprint" – the script.

But all of us are not working with Clients and Teams. In other words, "*What if all these people are ME?!?*" If you are your own Client and your own Team, I must quote the wisdom of Stan Lee: "With great power comes great responsibility."

The digital age has democratized all the tools of pre-production, production, and post-production. If your credit is Writer/Producer/Director/DP/Editor, and your equipment your smartphone, the production technology in that one device is beyond the imagination of Hollywood not so very long ago – and on less than the budget of a Hollywood day's catering. Even more amazingly, and even more crucially, it has also made worldwide distribution a possibility – thus the "viral video" phenomenon. This is the "power" of the proverb.

The "responsibility" is the flip side of this democratization. I'm afraid I must restate the cold hard facts of life I shared in Chapter 3. No one in the Audience cares if you are doing all the jobs yourself; *the Audience cares about what they see on their screens.* Anyone can catch lightning in a bottle and have *one* video go viral. The question is, "Can you do it twice?" You will have a much better chance of doing so as a one-person band if you have developed your skills in all the production crafts to the fullest of your ability. That is your responsibility to your Audience, and ultimately to yourself.

Another step toward fulfilling that responsibility is the development of a test audience. Especially if you are doing everything yourself, enlist a trusted friend or two to give you honest feedback at least in the writing and rough-cut stages. These advisors can help you see things that a full production team would . . . and to see them before you unleash your production on the world.

This leads to a final piece of good news – the best news of all, in fact. By taking the craft of screenwriting seriously, and by focusing on the final screened production from the first line that you write, you are taking the biggest step toward fulfilling your responsibility toward your Clients and your Audience.

Let's return to our musical analogy one more time. Once songwriters finish their work, they may record their song themselves, or they may send their composition to other musicians for the original recording. Whichever the choice, it will result in a different interpretation of that composition. If that first recording is a hit – and sometimes if it isn't – it will be picked up for a cover by yet another artist, and then another and another. Each singer and musician will bring their own interpretation to the composition. The Audience will react differently to each interpretation. *But it's still the same composition that is interpreted, and thus the heart of the Audience reaction.*

The old show-business saw "If it ain't on the page, it ain't on the stage" is an old saw because it's true. It's even more true when it comes to the screen. This can be wrapped up in two thoughts: think in terms of the final Audience experience, and remember the Audience are people just like you. In other words, write what you want to watch and hear on the screen. That's the heart of Applied Screenwriting.

Works Cited

Crowell, Thomas A. *The Pocket Lawyer for Filmmakers; A Legal Toolkit for Independent Producers*. 3rd ed., Routledge, 2022.

Dancyger, Ken, Jessie Keyt, and Jeff Rush. *Alternative Scriptwriting; Contemporary Storytelling for the Screen*. Routledge, 2023.

Dmytryk, Edward. *On Screen Writing*. Routledge, 2019.

Fink, Edward. *Dramatic Story Structure; A Primer for Screenwriters*. Routledge, 2014.

Stevens, Matt, and Claudia Hunter Johnson. *Script Partners; How to Succeed at Co-Writing for Film & TV*. Routledge, 2016.

APPENDIX 1

How to Format a Script . . . in the Form of a Script

Below is an example script that I have used for many semesters, in both graduate and undergraduate classes. Some of the information from the text is repeated for emphasis, but the focus of this script is setting up and writing a split-column in your own word processor.

THE SPLIT-COLUMN SCRIPT
By Dr. Carey Martin

VIDEO	AUDIO
1. WS-INT-CLASSROOM-DAY The writing students are listening to their instructor, DR. MARTIN.	1. MUSIC: "Smooth Jazz Instrumental" – FADE OUT after five seconds.
	DR MARTIN: What you have in your hands is an example of a split-column script. The content is directions to create a split-column script when working in Microsoft Word – the instructions assume you are already familiar with the program.
2. CU-INT-CLASSROOM-DAY DR. MARTIN crosses the room and sits down at a computer.	2. DR. MARTIN: The first thing we do is set the program to insert page numbers top right corner, and put the title of the piece and the name of the writer in the top center of the page.

VIDEO	AUDIO
3. MS-INT-CLASSROOM-DAY DR. MARTIN types at the computer as the class gather round to watch.	3. DR. MARTIN: We then insert a two-column table.
4. CU-INT-CLASSROOM-DAY The screen of the computer fills the screen.	4. DR. MARTIN (VO): Select the table, then turn "View Gridlines" on. Specify "Borders and Shading" to "None." Finally, turn "Numbers" within the table to "None."
5. MS-INT-CLASSROOM-DAY DR. MARTIN types at the computer as the class gather round to watch.	5. DR. MARTIN: Then type "VIDEO" in the left column top row. Tab over, and type "AUDIO" in the right column. The split-column script is called that because the information is organized into two columns. The left side is the video column; everything we will see in the finished piece. The right side is the audio column, everything we will hear in the piece.
6. CU - INT - CLASSROOM - DAY DR. MARTIN looks out at the class.	6. DR. MARTIN: Once we've labeled the columns, tab again to get into the left column. Here is where we write our shots. In a shooting script, every new row represents a new shot. And, every new shot begins with a shot header. From left to right, a shot header contains five elements.
7. CU-INT-CLASSROOM-DAY The computer screen shows a typical shot header.	7. DR. MARTIN: From left to right in the header, we have the Shot Number, the Frame Description, the Interior/Exterior designation, the Location, and the Day/Night designation. We've discussed all this in the text. Two brief reminders. First, if there's a roof overhead, it's an INT; if not, it's an EXT. Second, if you can see the sun, it's DAY; if not, it's NIGHT.

VIDEO	AUDIO
8. MS-INT-CLASSROOM-DAY DR. MARTIN turns to face the students; camera PANS with him as he does so, from his face to the faces of the students watching, and back to DR. MARTIN'S face again.	8. DR. MARTIN: Underneath the shot header is the shot description. This is what actually happens in the scene. Don't begin by writing "Shot of" or anything like that; just write what happens. You will notice that the scene description is in standard sentence case. Some writers use all caps for the description as well as the header. In my opinion this just makes the script harder to read, and it doesn't give you any real benefit, so I don't do it. The only information I put in all caps are the NAMES of all characters in the shot, and any essential CAMERA MOVES.
9. CU-INT-CLASSROOM-DAY JIM, a male student of traditional age, raises his hand.	9. JIM: When we go from one shot to the next, do we have to put cut to or anything like that?
10. OTS-INT-CLASSROOM-DAY (From over JIM's shoulder) DR. MARTIN nods.	10. DR. MARTIN: Good question. The answer is, not if you're just cutting from one shot to the next. The format uses cuts as the default transition. But, if you want a different transition –that is, something different to move from one shot to the next –
DISSOLVE TO:	
11. WS-INT-CLASSROOM-DAY The entire class is watching DR. MARTIN.	11. DR. MARTIN:– then you'd tab over to start a new row under the previous shot, write dissolve (or whatever transition you choose) TO, and tab again to start the next shot. Remember, if you're using a wipe or DVE, you need to specify what kind, as I have below.

VIDEO	AUDIO
DVE-PAGE TURN TO:	
12. CU-INT-CLASSROOM-DAY EVE, a female student of traditional age, raises her hand.	12. EVE: What about graphics? Like, if we wanted just the title on screen?
13. CU-INT-CLASSROOM-DAY DR. MARTIN smiles.	13. DR. MARTIN: That's also a good question.
14. GRAPHIC On a flaming background, "What about graphics?" appears in white letters.	14. DR. MARTIN (VO): First, type GRAPHIC in your shot header. Then, in your shot description, write what you want the graphic to look like. Oh, and jumping ahead to audio just a bit, you notice I put (VO) next to the character name in the dialogue, because I won't be physically present in the scene. VO is shot for Voice Over.
15. CU- INT-CLASSROOM-DAY EVE raises her hand again.	15. EVE: And if we wanted some graphics onscreen in the shot? I mean like in news, where they shot the reporter's name underneath them.
16. CU-INT-CLASSROOM-DAY DR. MARTIN nods again. CG: DR. CAREY MARTIN, lower quarter of screen.	16. DR. MARTIN: Good follow up. The best way is to use CG, which is short for Character Generator, followed by the information you want to show and the position on screen of the information. This can be anything, by the way: sports scores, titles, identifiers of the scene in news, any kind of information- you aren't limited to the talent's name.
17. CU-INT-CLASSROOM-DAY DR. MARTIN looks around the class.	17. DR. MARTIN: Any more questions about the video side?

VIDEO	AUDIO
18. WS-INT-CLASSROOM-DAY The students all shake their hands. DR. MARTIN turns back to the screen.	18. DR. MARTIN: Okay, moving on- the audio side is a little simpler. Of course you number the audio shot to match the video shot. Other than that, there are five things you can find in the audio column. The first is dialogue, which is anything a character says. Type the character's name in all caps, followed by a colon-
19. CU-INT-CLASSROOM-DAY DR. MARTIN types as he talks.	19. DR. MARTIN: - and then what he or she says in upper and lower case. If the dialogue continues between shots, use dashes at the point in the first shot where the cut should come, and at the beginning of the second shot, as I've done here. As I noted earlier, be conscious of the difference between Voice-Over and Off-Screen, as well.
	RAY (OS): What if you want the talent to talk in a certain way?
	DR. MARTIN (whispers): You mean like whispering? (normal voice) That's called dialogue directions, or parenthetical. You put them in parenthesis where the talent should begin. And don't put quotation marks around your dialogue, unless your character is quoting someone else. As you can see, there are no quotation marks around the dialogue in this example screenplay.
20. WS - INT - CLASSROOM - DAY The students are listening intently and looking at the class screen, where the script appears as DR. MARTIN types.	20. DR. MARTIN: Next, we can have music in a shot. Type MUSIC, all caps, followed by a colon, and then the type of music. The type can be very general, such as "classical music" or very specific, such as a particular song by ac certain artist.
	MUSIC: "Smooth Jazz Instrumental" UNDER.

VIDEO	AUDIO
21. CU - INT - CLASSROOM - DAY DR. MARTIN double-checks to make sure he's playing public domain music.	21. DR. MARTIN: If the music just starts at full volume, that's all you need to do. Use the term "Under" to indicate that the music continues playing, but not so loudly that it drowns out the dialogue.
22. WS - INT - CLASSROOM - DAY DR. MARTIN indicates the appropriate parts of the script on the screen.	22. DR. MARTIN: The music starts when you place it in the script. You indicate where it stops in one of three ways. You may write how many seconds you want to use of the music. You can write the verse that the music should come in, and the verse where it goes out. Or you can write another cue in the script at the point where the music comes out. MUSIC: "Smooth Jazz Instrumental" OUT. DR. MARTIN: Notice I skip a line between every audio element. This makes the script easier to read.
23. CU-INT-CLASSROOM-DAY JIM raises his hand again.	23. JIM: What if you want music to continue over several shots?
23. CU-INT-CLASSROOM-DAY DR. MARTIN smiles.	22. DR. MARTIN: Write MUSIC CONTINUES in each shot after the first. MUSIC: "Classical Instrumental"
24. WS-INT-CLASSROOM-DAY The class listens to the music.	24. MUSIC CONTINUES
25. CU-INT-CLASSROOM-DAY DR. MARTIN nods as the music stops.	25. MUSIC OUT DR. MARTIN: It's that simple.
26. OTS-INT-CLASSROOM-DAY (From over DR. MARTIN'S shoulder) JIM still has a puzzled look.	26. JIM: Is there a special order that you have to put your audio elements in?

VIDEO	AUDIO
27. MS-INT-CLASSROOM-DAY DR. MARTIN looks up at the student.	27. DR. MARTIN: Yes, the audio goes in the order that it happens in the shot. Now, the next type of audio is the sound effect.
	SFX: a door SLAMS.
DR. MARTIN glances in the direction of the door, smiles, and continues.	DR. MARTIN: The sound effect is any noise that is neither dialogue nor music, but which has to happen at a particular point in the script – because characters react to that. The abbreviation SFX designates sounds effect, and the sound itself is in all caps.
28. WS-INT-CLASSROOM-DAY DR. MARTIN gets up, steps away from the desk, and smiles.	28. DR. MARTIN: The last kind of sound in the audio is what is variously called ambient, background, or nat- short for natural- sound. This is the sound that occurs naturally in the scene. I'll stop for a moment so you can hear.
29. WS-INT-CLASSROOM-DAY The students listen carefully.	29. NAT SOUND (3 seconds).
30. CU-INT- CLASSROOM-DAY DR. MARTIN continues.	30. DR. MARTIN: If all I want is this sound in a scene, I write NAT SOUND. Other writers use AMBIENT or BACKGROUND to mean the same thing. Notice I also include the time of the shot. All shots with dialogue are timed by however long it takes to say the dialogue. All shots with no dialogue have to have the time included in the script. Since there's no verbal cue for the editor, she or he has to know how long to let the shot run.
31. CU-INT-CLASSROOM-DAY ANA, a female student somewhat younger than the others, raises her hand.	31. ANA: What if you want nat sound, but you also want the talent's voice?

VIDEO	AUDIO
32. CU-INT-CLASSROOM-DAY DR. MARTIN grins broadly.	32. DR. MARTIN: Well, if the talent is recording the audio on location, Nat sound is automatically in the shot. But, if you want the talent to do a voice-over for a shot with Nat sound-
33. WS-EXT-CLASSROOM-DAY Birds are sitting on the windowsill, chirping to each other.	33. NAT SOUND: Birds chirping (2 seconds). DR. MARTIN (VO-NAT):-then indicate that by first describing the nat sound, then putting (VO-NAT) after the talent's name in the dialogue, which indicates you hear both at the same time. You may include a description of what exactly the nat sound is, at your option, as I've done here.
34. CU-INT-CLASSROOM-DAY EVE raises her hand again	34. EVE: You said there were five things you can find in the audio column, but nat sound only makes four, and you said that was the last.
35. CU-INT-CLASSROOM-DAY DR. MARTIN chuckles.	35. DR. MARTIN: Very good! The last thing you find in the audio column is the rarest. That's SILENCE- no recorded sound at all.
36. WS-INT-CLASSROOM-DAY The students listen carefully.	36. SILENCE
37. MS-INT-CLASSROOM-DAY DR. MARTIN stands up and faces the class.	37. DR. MARTIN: As you can hear, there's a world of difference between that and a nat sound where no one is talking. Now, you'll notice that I skip a line at the end of every shot, whether the audio or the video is longer. That makes the script more readable.
38. CU-INT-CLASSROOM-DAY ANA raises her hand again.	38. ANA: I have one more question. You talked about video transitions. Are there any audio transitions?

VIDEO	AUDIO
39. CU-INT-CLASSROOM-DAY DR. MARTIN nods.	39. DR. MARTIN: Yes, but only three. The default is a cut-one sounds stops and the next begins. A sound can also FADE IN, going from zero volume to full, or FADE OUT from full volume to zero. Finally there's a SEGUE, in which one sound fades out as the other fades in. MUSIC: "Scotland the Brave," on bagpipes, FADES IN, 10 seconds. SEGUE TO: MUSIC: "Greensleeves," on harp, 10 seconds, FADES OUTS. DR. MARTIN: And, if there aren't any other questions about audio, that about wraps it up.
40. CU-INT-CLASSROOM-DAY JIM raises his hand again.	40. JIM: Excuse me, Dr. Martin, but say I've got a video clip that I've already shot, or somebody else already shot, and I want to use it in my script. How do I script that?
41. WS-EXT-OUTERSPACE-DAY The earth, shot from the Moon, peacefully rotates in space (from NASA stock footage). CG: The Earth from the Moon, courtesy NASA.	41. DR. MARTIN (VO): Script it just like you would any other shot. You can indicate in the scene description that it's from an earlier source, such as news tapes, stock footage, or the like, as I have here with this shot of the Earth from the Moon, but it's not necessary. That's a wrap, guys – thanks, and have a great day!
42. WS-INT-CLASSROOM-DAY JIM, RAY, EVE and ANA and the other students file out as DR. MARTIN begins collecting his materials.	42. MUSIC: "LU Alma Mater"- FADE OUT after five seconds.

APPENDIX 2

The Narrative, the Split-Column, and the North Star

The following two items illustrate how each format will work in an Applied Screenwriting situation. My goal is to write an instructional video demonstrating two valid step-by-step processes to achieve the desired "North Star" result. I have three requirements. First, I am limited to one location. Second, our dauntless hero and our intrepid heroine, Jack and Jill, are the stars of the production. Third, it should simulate and parody the three-camera, studio audience cooking show.

Below is a narrative screenplay that we might write on commission for a Producer and a Director to produce with their Team.

```
FADE IN:
INT. JACK AND JILL KITCHEN - DAY
A modern, well-equipped kitchen; well-lit and scrupulously
clean, with ample cabinets behind a cooking island. Shining
utensils and measuring cups are laid out on the counter.
Steam rises from one large pot and one smaller pot, while
on the grill portion, a hot dog sizzles. Upbeat and cheery
generic TV music plays.

                    ANNOUNCER (V.O.)
              And now, ladies and gentlemen -
              Welcome to Jack and Jill COOK!

The unseen Audience applauds.
JACK, a sturdy, clean-cut lad whose good looks are only
slightly marred by a tasteful head bandage, and JILL, an
athletic, adventurous young woman with oft-signed casts on
```

both wrists, walk into the kitchen through the back door. Both are dressed in casual clothes covered by professional aprons. Jack is also wearing cooking gloves. They smile at each other and then at the audience.

> JACK
> Hi, I'm Jack!

> JILL
> And I'm Jill! Welcome to the very first episode of our new show!

The unseen Audience applauds.

> JACK
> As you all may know, our old show, Jack and Jill Climb Hills, well –

> JILL
> It didn't turn out so well. But we're both doing much better, thanks!

The unseen Audience applauds again.

> JACK
> Yes, the doctors say we're both fine. Really.

> JILL
> And we're so grateful to the network for giving us another chance!

> JACK
> You bet, Jill! Now, today we're tackling something simple –

> JILL
> At the network's request!

The unseen Audience laughs.

> JACK
> Yes, at their special request. Any who, today we're going to show you how to make a hot dog!

> JILL
> Now, we know what you're saying! Everybody knows how to make a hot dog!

```
                    JACK
          Sure, you boil it in your favorite
          Hops-based adult beverage!

Jill gives Jack a look.

                    JACK
          What? The network wants us to stay
          "Family Friendly."

                    JILL
          What - no, I know what you meant. But
          that's not how you make a hot dog.
          You grill it. Everybody knows that.

                    JACK
          That's how you make your hot dog.

                    JILL
          I can't believe I just learned this
          about you.

                    JACK
          Look, the whole point is we're each
          going to build our dog our way, right?
          So I cooked it my way, too.

                    JILL
          OK, fine. So, anyway, we've COOKED
          our hot dogs - now we're going to
          MAKE them.

                    JACK
          Exactly! Step by step, the Jack and
          Jill way! Now, ladies first -

                    JILL
          Oh no, Jack, you go first. Please.

                    JACK
          Well, if you insist!
```

Jack opens a cabinet on his side of the kitchen. He removes a plate and a package of plain white hot dog buns, placing each on the counter in front of him. He reaches into his drawer and extracts a pair of tongs, setting them next to the plate. He turns to the refrigerator on his side and removes a standard red bottle of ketchup and an equally standard yellow bottle of mustard. With pride, he arranges them in a pleasing formation next to plate, buns, and tongs. Then he takes a single bun from the package, places exactly in the center of the plate, and begins to squirt ketchup onto the bun.

                    JILL
          What are you doing?

                    JACK
          What do you mean?

                    JILL
          What. Are. You. Doing?

                    JACK
          What does it look like? I'm putting
          ketchup on my hot dog.

                    JILL
          No you're not!

Jack pauses and gives her a look.

                    JACK
          Ah, honey, I'm the one who had the
          head injury –

                    JILL
          You are not putting ketchup on a
          hot dog, you're putting ketchup on
          a bun!

                    JACK
          And?

                    JILL
          You dress the hot dog, not the bun!
          Everybody knows that!

                    JACK
          I didn't, and I'm part of everybody.

                    JILL
          Ok. Fine.

Jack nods. He squirts even more ketchup onto the bun. Jill stares, almost slack-jawed. Jack then squirts an equal amount of mustard. He takes the tongs and, with a flourish, uses them to extract a single hot dog from the steaming pot. He carefully places the wiener in the center of the bun, lays down the tongs, and presents the result with an even more proud flourish to the audience.

The unseen Audience applauds enthusiastically.

The sound of the applause snaps Jill out of her daze.

                    JILL
          That's IT? That's ALL? THAT'S
          HOW YOU BUILD A HOT DOG?!?

Jack nods in honest bewilderment. Jill shakes her head again.

                    JILL
        No wonder you cook in beer.

As Jill stares sadly at his result, Jack winks at the audience.

                    JACK
        All right, honey, it's your turn.
        Let's see how you do it.

                    JILL
        Oh, gladly.

Jack makes a go-ahead motion. Jill doesn't move.

                    JACK
        It's all yours.

Jill lifts her cast-bound wrists.

                    JACK
        Oh. Right. Sorry.

Jack moves into position to help. Jill smiles her thanks.

                    JILL
        OK, the grilled hot dog is ready.

                    JACK
        The buns are right –

                    JILL
        No. Please get the sweet
        Hawaiian style rolls from the
        top cabinet, dear.

Jack reaches up, opens the cabinet, and gets the rolls. He glances at the price tag and does a double take.

                    JACK
        These cost more than all my stuff
        put together.

                    JILL
        Really? Now the plate, please.

Jack gets a plate and puts it in front of Jill. Thinking quickly, he opens the buns, puts one on the plate, picks up the grilled hot dog with the tongs, and puts it on the bun.

                    JILL
        Oh, thank you, sweetheart! Now we
        need the ketchup and the mustard –

Jack reaches for both.

>   JILL
>   No, sweetheart, the German Curry
>   ketchup and the Sweet Onion Mustard.
>   In the refrigerator.

>   JACK
>   Oh - kay . . .

Jack gets both bottles from Jill's refrigerator. Jill nods in approval as Jack returns to his spot.

>   JILL
>   Now, we carefully place a stripe
>   of mustard, then a drizzle of
>   ketchup, directly on the wiener.

Jack hesitates.

>   JILL
>   Go ahead, Jack.

With the greatest of care, Jack lays down a neat band of mustard directly on the hot dog. As Jill nods, he then places a surgically precise z-line of ketchup.

>   JILL
>   Very good, dear!

The unseen Audience applauds enthusiastically.

>   JACK
>   Well, I guess that wraps -

>   JILL
>   Wraps?

>   JACK
>   There's more?

>   JILL
>   Of course there's more! Next
>   comes the relish. My fave
>   is the sweet onion.

Jack takes his cue, gets the relish from the refrigerator.

>   JILL
>   Three tablespoons, evenly spaced.

Jack opens the jar, takes a measuring tablespoon, and applies three scoops.

>   JILL
>   Just like that. Now the first layer
>   of cheese.

                    JACK
          The first layer?

                    JILL
          Certainly.

Jack takes a moment to check the price tags on the German
curry ketchup, sweet onion mustard, and sweet onion relish.

                    JACK
          Did we clear this with the Production
          Budget?

                    JILL
          Oh, sweetheart, you're such a kidder.
          First layer of cheese, please.

Jack looks in JILL's refrigerator.

                    JACK
          That would be the mild cheddar.
          Right?

                    JILL
          Exactly! It's a nice subtle balance,
          and kind of a firm foundation.

                    JACK
          A firm –

                    JILL
          A third of a cup to a half cup,
          spread evenly over the hot dog.

                    JACK
          Can some get on the bun too?

                    JILL
          A little.

Jack takes the measuring cup, fills it with mild cheddar, and
applies it to the dog as Jill watches carefully.

                    JACK
          Like so?

                    JILL
          Just like so!

The unseen Audience applauds enthusiastically.

                    JILL
          Now, my own personal chili!

                    JACK
          And folks, you're going to want
          to tune in when Jill makes that!
          Can you give them a hint, honey?

```
Jill blushes a little.

                    JILL
          Oh, it's basically just ground
          beef, black beans, kidney beans,
          red beans, Vidalia onions, San
          Marzano tomatoes, green chilis,
          and my blend of spices. But
          that's next week.

Jill indicates the larger steaming pot.

                    JILL
          Two ladles full, if you please!

Jack ladles out two heaping helpings. The hot dog almost
disappears.

                    JILL
          Now a sprinkling of fresh cut
          Vidalias!

                    JACK
          Uh, Jill?

                    JILL
          Yes Jack?

                    JACK
          The relish is onion. The mustard
          is onion flavored. And, if memory
          serves, the chili has plenty of
          onions too.

                    JILL
          That cracked crown didn't affect
          your memory, sweetheart.

The unseen Audience chuckles.

                    JACK
          Does it really need more onions?

                    JILL
          Oh come on, Jack, people love onions!

Jill makes a sweeping gesture to the unseen Audience.

                    JILL
          Who loves onions out there?!?

The unseen Audience cheers.

                    JACK
          Oh - kay.
```

He gets the freshly chopped Vidalia onions from the
refrigerator.

>   JILL
>   Just a sprinkling. We don't want
>   to overdo it.

Jack gives Jill a look. Jill smiles at him sweetly. He
sprinkles the chopped onions. Jill nods approvingly.

>   JILL
>   Now the second layer of cheese.
>   You might have to look for this,
>   but Honey Siracha Gouda is so worth
>   it!

Jack retrieves the grated Honey Siracha Gouda from the
refrigerator.

>   JACK
>   A third of a cup to a half cup?

>   JILL
>   A third of a cup to a half cup!

Jack lays on the second layer of cheese as Jill watches
approvingly.

>   JILL
>   We're in the home stretch, now!
>   A quick sprinkling of roasted
>   Garlic sauerkraut . . .

Jack starts to go back to the refrigerator, then spots the
unopened jar on the counter.

>   JACK
>   That's right, you don't have to
>   refrigerate till you open it.

Jack picks up the jar, notes the price, shrugs in
resignation, and opens it.

>   JILL
>   Another light sprinkle, please.

Jack complies.

>   JILL
>   And now, the finale. I picked
>   up this tip from our friends down
>   South. The slaw!

Jack gets the slaw from the refrigerator.

>   JACK
>   Now, this recipe came from my
>   Grandmother. It's a vinegar
>   based slaw, no mayo. Really
>   crisp and refreshing.

>   JILL
>   She gave us her secret recipe
>   in needlepoint for our
>   wedding present!

The unseen Audience gives a collective "Awww."

>   JILL
>   You finish it off, sweetheart.
>   As much as your heart desires.
>   In fact, you can SLAW-ter it!

The unseen Audience laughs. Jack grins.

>   JACK
>   Don't encourage her.

He puts on a reasonable amount of slaw. Hot dog and bun have completely vanished beneath the heap of additions. Realization sets in as Jill stares at the concoction.

>   JILL
>   Ah . . . did you remember the knives and
>   forks?

>   JACK
>   You can't use a knife and fork on a
>   hot dog. You eat franks with your
>   hands. Everybody –

>   JILL
>   Yeah, yeah, everybody knows that.

Jill looks at the hot dog, looks at her wrists. Her expression is pure hunger.

Jack reaches out and very carefully scoops up the monster dog in his gloved hands. He holds it gently at the perfect level for Jill to take a bite. Jill looks adoringly at Jack. She takes a bite. Her face shows pure bliss. Jack braces himself and takes a bite himself. His face lights up with surprise, then enjoyment.

>   JILL
>   I love you, Jack.

Appendix 2: The Narrative, the Split-Column, and the North Star **139**

```
                JACK
        I love you too, Jill. That's it
        for today, folks - we'll see you
        next time!
                JILL
        And remember - keep cooking for
        love, and you'll keep loving
        to cook!
The unseen Audience cheers uproariously.
                                           FADE OUT
```

As I've noted in the text, whatever you think of the creativity of characters and plot, this leaves all the production creative choices in the hands of the Production Team – and as I've also noted, this is exactly as it should be. I did my best to imply my ideas on cinematography, editing, and the like, but that's all I – or any screenwriter – can do.

Now, in the split-column script, I will write exactly how I see the production unfolding in my head. For good or ill, the implicit will be explicit. As I mentioned, this is my favored format for Applied Screenwriting, especially when I am Producer and Director as well. Two notes: first, the entire piece can be shot single camera; second, the "Audience" can be created with sound effects from a digital library. It looks like this:

VIDEO	AUDIO
1. MWS - INT. JACK AND JILL KITCHEN - DAY A modern, well-equipped kitchen; well-lit and scrupulously clean, with ample cabinets behind a cooking island. Shining utensils and measuring cups are laid out on the counter.	1. MUSIC: Upbeat and cheery generic TV music plays.
2. MCU - INT. JACK AND JILL KITCHEN - DAY Steam rises from one large pot and one smaller pot, while on the grill portion, a hot dog sizzles. CG: Jack and Jill COOK!	2. MUSIC: CONTINUES UNDER ANNOUNCER (V.O.): And now, ladies and gentlemen - Welcome to Jack and Jill COOK! SFX: The unseen Audience applauds.

VIDEO	AUDIO
3. WS - INT. JACK AND JILL KITCHEN - DAY JACK, a sturdy, clean-cut lad whose good looks are only slightly marred by a tasteful head bandage, and JILL, an athletic, adventurous young woman with oft-signed casts on both wrists, walk into the kitchen through the back door. Both are dressed in casual clothes covered by professional aprons. Jack is also wearing cooking gloves.	3. MUSIC: CONTINUES UNDER AND OUT JACK: Hi, I'm Jack! JILL: And I'm Jill! Welcome to the very first episode of our new show! SFX: The unseen Audience applauds.
4. MWS - INT. JACK AND JILL KITCHEN - DAY JACK and JILL smile at each other and then at the audience as the camera DOLLIES in to a Medium 2-Shot.	4. JACK: As you all may know, our old show, Jack and Jill Climb Hills, well - JILL: It didn't turn out so well. But we're both doing much better, thanks! SFX: The unseen Audience applauds.
5. MCU - INT. JACK AND JILL KITCHEN - DAY JACK gives a plucky grin.	5. JACK: Yes, the doctors say we're both fine. Really.
6. MCU - INT. JACK AND JILL KITCHEN - DAY JILL smiles winningly.	6. JILL: And we're so grateful to the network for giving us another chance!
7. MS - INT. JACK AND JILL KITCHEN - DAY JACK and JILL settle in behind the counter.	7. JACK: You bet, Jill! Now, today we're tackling something simple - JILL: At the network's request! SFX: The unseen Audience laughs. JACK: Yes, at their special request. Any who, today we're going to show you how to make a hot dog!

VIDEO	AUDIO
8. MCU - INT. JACK AND JILL KITCHEN - DAY JILL addresses the camera.	8. JILL: Now, we know what you're saying! Everybody knows how to make a hot dog!
9. MCU - INT. JACK AND JILL KITCHEN - DAY JACK addresses the camera.	9. JACK: Sure, you boil it in your favorite Hops-based adult beverage!
10. MS - INT. JACK AND JILL KITCHEN - DAY JILL give JACK a look. JACK returns the look puzzledly.	10. JACK: What? The network wants us to stay "Family Friendly." JILL: What - no, I know what you meant. But that's not how you make a hot dog. You grill it. Everybody knows that. JACK: That's how you make your hot dog.
11. MCU - INT. JACK AND JILL KITCHEN - DAY JILL shakes her head as she addresses JACK.	11. JILL: I can't believe I just learned this about you.
12. MCU - INT. JACK AND JILL KITCHEN - DAY JACK gives JILL a cheerful grin.	12. JACK: Look, the whole point is we're each going to build our dog our way, right? So, I cooked it my way, too.
12. MWS - INT. JACK AND JILL KITCHEN - DAY JILL gives the camera an aside glance of mock frustration, then smiles at JACK, who returns the smile readily. He makes a gallant gesture to Jill to go first as he speaks. Jill returns the gesture with good humor.	12. JILL: OK, fine. So, anyway, we've COOKED our hot dogs - now we're going to MAKE them. JACK: Exactly! Step by step, the Jack and Jill way! Now, ladies first - JILL: Oh no, Jack, you go first. Please. JACK: Well, if you insist!

VIDEO	AUDIO
13. FS - INT. JACK AND JILL KITCHEN - DAY	13. MUSIC: Upbeat and cheery generic TV music plays.
Camera TRUCKS with JACK as Jack opens a cabinet on his side of the kitchen. He removes a plate and a package of plain white hot dog buns, placing each on the counter in front of him. He reaches into his drawer and extracts a pair of tongs, setting them next to the plate. He turns to the refrigerator on his side and removes a standard red bottle of ketchup and an equally standard yellow bottle of mustard.	NAT SOUND: UNDER
14. MCU - INT. JACK AND JILL KITCHEN - DAY	14. MUSIC: CONTINUES2
	NAT SOUND: UNDER
With pride, JACK arranges the condiments in a pleasing formation next to plate, buns, and tongs. Then he takes a single bun from the package, places exactly in the center of the plate, and begins to squirt ketchup onto the bun.	
15. CU - INT. JACK AND JILL KITCHEN - DAY	15: MUSIC: OUT
	JILL: What are you doing?
JILL reacts in horror.	
16. MS - INT. JACK AND JILL KITCHEN - DAY	16. JACK: What do you mean?
JACK stops in his tracks, looking quizzically at JILL.	JILL: What. Are. You. Doing?
	JACK: What does it look like? I'm putting ketchup on my hot dog.

VIDEO	AUDIO
17. MCU - INT. JACK AND JILL KITCHEN - DAY JILL is still staring in horror.	17. JILL: No you're not!
18. MCU - INT. JACK AND JILL KITCHEN - DAY JACK looks at JILL with some concern.	18. JACK: Ah, honey, I'm the one who had the head injury –
19. MS - INT. JACK AND JILL KITCHEN - DAY JILL points at the beginning of JACK's work. JACK looks at her in befuddlement.	19. JILL: You are not putting ketchup on a hot dog, you're putting ketchup on a bun! JACK: And? JILL: You dress the hot dog, not the bun! Everybody knows that!
20. MCU - INT. JACK AND JILL KITCHEN - DAY JACK shrugs innocently.	20. JACK: I didn't, and I'm part of everybody.
21. MS - INT. JACK AND JILL KITCHEN - DAY JILL throws up her hands as she speaks. JACK nods in response.	21. JILL: OK. Fine.
22. CU - INT. JACK AND JILL KITCHEN - DAY BIRD'S EYE view as JACK squirts an intimidating amount of ketchup on the bun. Jack then squirts an equal amount of mustard.	22. MUSIC: Upbeat and cheery generic TV music plays. NAT SOUND: UNDER
23. CU - INT. JACK AND JILL KITCHEN - DAY JILL stares, almost slack-jawed.	23. MUSIC: CONTINUES NAT SOUND: UNDER

VIDEO	AUDIO
24. MS - INT. JACK AND JILL KITCHEN - DAY JACK takes the tongs and, with a flourish, uses them to extract a single hot dog from the steaming pot.	24. MUSIC: CONTINUES NAT SOUND: UNDER
25. CU - INT. JACK AND JILL KITCHEN - DAY BIRD'S EYE view as JACK carefully places the wiener in the center of the bun.	25. MUSIC: CONTINUES NAT SOUND: UNDER
26. MS - INT. JACK AND JILL KITCHEN - DAY JACK lays down the tongs and presents the result with an even more proud flourish to the audience.	26. MUSIC: CONTINUES SFX: The unseen Audience applauds.
27. CU - INT. JACK AND JILL KITCHEN - DAY The sound of the applause snaps JILL out of her daze.	27. JILL: That's IT? That's ALL? THAT'S HOW YOU BUILD A HOT DOG?!?
28. CU - INT. JACK AND JILL KITCHEN - DAY JACK nods in honest bewilderment.	28. NAT SOUND
29. CU - INT. JACK AND JILL KITCHEN - DAY JILL shakes her head again.	29. JILL: No wonder you cook in beer.
30. MS - INT. JACK AND JILL KITCHEN - DAY As JILL stares at his result, JACK winks at the audience. JACK makes a go-ahead motion. JILL doesn't move.	30. JACK: All right, honey, it's your turn. Let's see how you do it. JILL: Oh, gladly. JACK: It's all yours.

VIDEO	AUDIO
31. MCU - INT. JACK AND JILL KITCHEN - DAY	31. NAT SOUND
JILL lifts her cast-bound wrists.	
32. MS - INT. JACK AND JILL KITCHEN - DAY	32. JACK: Oh. Right. Sorry.
JACK moves into position to help.	JILL: OK, the grilled hot dog is ready.
JILL smiles her thanks.	JACK: The buns are right –
	JILL: No. Please get the sweet Hawaiian style rolls from the top cabinet, dear.
33. MCU - INT. JACK AND JILL KITCHEN - DAY	33. JACK: These cost more than all my stuff put together.
Camera PANS with JACK as he reaches up, opens the cabinet, and gets the rolls. He glances at the price tag and does a double take.	
34. MCU - INT. JACK AND JILL KITCHEN - DAY	34. JILL: Really? Now the plate, please.
JILL smiles innocently.	
35. MS - INT. JACK AND JILL KITCHEN - DAY	35. JILL: Oh, thank you, sweetheart! Now we need the ketchup and the mustard –
JACK gets a plate and puts it in front of JILL. Thinking quickly, he opens the buns, puts one on the plate, picks up the grilled hot dog with the tongs, and puts it on the bun.	No, sweetheart, the German Curry Ketchup and the Sweet Onion Mustard. In the refrigerator.
At his cue, Jack reaches for both ketchup and mustard.	JACK: Oh – kay . . .

146 Appendix 2: The Narrative, the Split-Column, and the North Star

VIDEO	AUDIO
36. MCU – INT. JACK AND JILL KITCHEN – DAY Camera PANS with JACK as he gets both bottles from Jill's refrigerator.	36. NAT SOUND
37. MS – INT. JACK AND JILL KITCHEN – DAY JILL nods in approval as JACK returns to his spot. Jack hesitates.	37. JILL: Now, we carefully place a stripe of mustard, then a drizzle of ketchup, directly on the wiener . . . Go ahead, Jack.
38. CU – INT. JACK AND JILL KITCHEN – DAY BIRD'S EYE view as JACK, with the greatest of care, lays down a neat band of mustard directly on the hot dog. He then places a surgically precise z-line of ketchup.	38. JILL (O.S.): Very good, dear! SFX: The unseen Audience applauds enthusiastically.
39. MS – INT. JACK AND JILL KITCHEN – DAY JACK smiles at JILL, then at the camera. JILL smiles at the camera, then at Jack. Jack takes his cue, gets the relish from the refrigerator.	39. JACK: Well, I guess that wraps – JILL: Wraps? JACK: There's more? JILL: Of course there's more! Next comes the relish. My fave is the sweet onion.
40. MCU – INT. JACK AND JILL KITCHEN – DAY BIRD'S EYE view as JACK opens the jar, takes a measuring tablespoon, and applies three scoops.	40. JILL (O.S.): Three tablespoons, evenly spaced.

VIDEO	AUDIO
41. MS - INT. JACK AND JILL KITCHEN - DAY JILL smiles her approval again. JACK takes a moment to check the price tags on the German Curry Ketchup, Sweet Onion Mustard, and Sweet Onion Relish.	41. JILL: Just like that. Now the first layer of cheese. JACK: The first layer? JILL: Certainly. JACK: Did we clear this with the Production Budget? JILL: Oh, sweetheart, you're such a kidder. First layer of cheese, please.
42. MCU - INT. JACK AND JILL KITCHEN - DAY Camera PANS with JACK as he looks in Jill's refrigerator.	42. JACK: That would be the mild cheddar. Right?
42. MWS - INT. JACK AND JILL KITCHEN - DAY JILL nods enthusiastically. JACK retrieves the cheese and returns to the counter.	JILL: Exactly! It's a nice subtle balance, and kind of a firm foundation. JACK: A firm - JILL: A third of a cup to a half cup, spread evenly over the hot dog. JACK: Can some get on the bun too? JILL: A little.
43. CU - INT. JACK AND JILL KITCHEN - DAY BIRD'S EYE view as JACK takes the measuring cup, fills it with mild cheddar, and applies it to the dog.	43. JACK: Like so?

148 Appendix 2: The Narrative, the Split-Column, and the North Star

VIDEO	AUDIO
44. MS - INT. JACK AND JILL KITCHEN - DAY JILL nods enthusiastically.	44. JILL: Just like so! SFX: The unseen Audience applauds enthusiastically.
45. MCU - INT. JACK AND JILL KITCHEN - DAY JILL smiles at the audience.	45. JILL: Now my own personal chili!
46. MCU - INT. JACK AND JILL KITCHEN - DAY JACK smiles at the camera.	46. JACK: And folks, you're going to want to tune in when Jill makes that! Can you give them a hint, honey?
47. MCU - INT. JACK AND JILL KITCHEN - DAY JILL blushes a little.	45. JILL: Oh, it's basically just ground beef, black beans, kidney beans, red beans, Vidalia onions, San Marzano tomatoes, green chilis, and my blend of spices. But that's next week.
48. MS - INT. JACK AND JILL KITCHEN - DAY JILL indicates the larger steaming pot. JACK ladles out two heaping helpings. The hot dog almost disappears. Jack pauses; as he begins the exchange with Jill, the camera DOLLIES in to a MC 2-shot of them. On her cue, Jill makes a sweeping gesture to the unseen Audience.	48. JILL: Two ladles, if you please . . . ! Now a sprinkling of fresh cut Vidalias! JACK: Uh, Jill? JILL: Yes Jack? JACK: The relish is onion. The mustard is onion flavored. And, if memory serves, the chili has plenty of onions too. JILL: That cracked crown didn't affect your memory, sweetheart. SFX: The unseen Audience chuckles.

VIDEO	AUDIO
	JACK: Does it really need more onions?
	JILL: Oh come on, Jack, people love onions! Who loves onions out there?!?
	SFX: The unseen Audience cheers.
49. MCU - INT. JACK AND JILL KITCHEN - DAY Camera PANS with JACK as he gets the freshly chopped Vidalia onions from Jill's refrigerator.	49. JACK: Oh - kay.
50. MS - INT. JACK AND JILL KITCHEN - DAY On her line, JACK gives JILL a look. Jill smiles at him sweetly. He sprinkles the chopped onions.	50. JILL: Just a sprinkling. We don't want to overdo it.
51. MCU - INT. JACK AND JILL KITCHEN - DAY JILL nods approvingly.	51. JILL: Now the second layer of cheese. You might have to look for this, but Honey Siracha Gouda is so worth it!
52. MS - INT. JACK AND JILL KITCHEN - DAY JACK retrieves the grated Honey Siracha Gouda from the refrigerator. He lays on the second layer of cheese as JILL watches approvingly. Jack starts to go back to the refrigerator, then spots the unopened jar on the counter. He picks up the jar, notes the price, shrugs in resignation, and opens it.	52. JACK: A third of a cup to a half cup? JILL: A third of a cup to a half cup! (pauses) We're in the home stretch, now! A quick sprinkling of roasted Garlic sauerkraut . . . JACK: That's right, you don't have to refrigerate till you open it. JILL: Another light sprinkle, please.

VIDEO	AUDIO
53. CU - INT. JACK AND JILL KITCHEN - DAY BIRD'S EYE view as JACK complies.	53. NAT SOUND
54. MS - INT. JACK AND JILL KITCHEN - DAY As JILL speaks, JACK gets the slaw from the refrigerator.	54. JILL: And now, the finale. I picked up this tip from our friends down South. The slaw! JACK: Now, this recipe came from my Grandmother. It's a vinegar based slaw, no mayo. Really crisp and refreshing. JILL: She gave us her secret recipe in needlepoint for our wedding present! SFX: The unseen Audience gives a collective "Aww."
55. CU - INT. JACK AND JILL KITCHEN - DAY JILL addresses JACK.	55. JILL: You finish it off, sweetheart. As much as your heart desires. In fact, you can SLAW-ter it! SFX: The unseen Audience laughs.
56. CU - INT. JACK AND JILL KITCHEN - DAY JACK grins and addresses the Audience.	56. JACK: Don't encourage her.
57. MS - INT. JACK AND JILL KITCHEN - DAY JACK puts on a reasonable amount of slaw.	57. MUSIC: triumphant classical UNDER, then UP

VIDEO	AUDIO
58. CU - INT. JACK AND JILL KITCHEN - DAY Hot dog and bun have completely vanished beneath the heap of additions.	58. MUSIC: triumphant classical flourish FULL, then OUT
59. CU - INT. JACK AND JILL KITCHEN - DAY Realization sets in as JILL stares at the concoction.	59. JILL: Ah . . . did you remember the knives and forks?
60. CU - INT. JACK AND JILL KITCHEN - DAY JACK smiles broadly.	60. JACK: You can't use a knife and fork on a hot dog. You eat franks with your hands. Everybody -
61. MS - INT. JACK AND JILL KITCHEN - DAY JILL looks at the hot dog, looks at her wrists. Her expression is pure hunger. JACK reaches out and very carefully scoops up the monster dog in his gloved hands. He holds it gently at the perfect level for Jill to take a bite. Jill looks adoringly at Jack, and takes a bite.	61. JILL: Yeah, yeah, everybody knows that. MUSIC: romantic classical UNDER and UP FULL.
62. CU - INT. JACK AND JILL KITCHEN - DAY JILL'S face shows pure bliss.	62. MUSIC CONTINUES
63. CU - INT. JACK AND JILL KITCHEN - DAY JACK braces himself and takes a bite himself. His face lights up with surprise, then enjoyment.	63. MUSIC CONTINUES

VIDEO	AUDIO
64. MS - INT. JACK AND JILL KITCHEN - DAY JILL, still blissful, turns to JACK as he turns to her. On Jack's second line, they turn back to the Audience.	64. MUSIC: romantic classical fades UNDER, SEGUE to upbeat and cheery generic TV music UNDER. JILL: I love you, Jack. JACK: I love you too, Jill. That's it for today, folks - we'll see you next time! JILL: And remember - keep cooking for love, and you'll keep loving to cook! SFX: The unseen Audience cheers uproariously.
DISSOLVE TO:	
65. GRAPHIC On sky blue background, dark rose script, "Jack and Jill Cook!"	65. MUSIC: upbeat and cheery generic TV music UP FULL and OUT.

APPENDIX 3

Watching to Listen – A Filmography of Dialogue

As promised in Chapter 8, following is my personal list of movies to study for how the Characters talk. Of course, all have many other delights to appreciate, and equally obviously none are "Applied Screenwriting." Two great things about drawing dialogue inspiration (not plagiarism!) from features to our humbler endeavors, though; it costs nothing, and it works.

Works Cited

Airplane! Written & Directed by Jim Abrahams, David Zucker, and Jerry Zucker, Paramount Pictures, 1980.

The Avengers. Written by Joss Whedon and Zak Penn, Directed by Joss Whedon, Marvel Studios, 2012.

Blade Runner. Written by Hampton Fancher and David Peoples from the Novel by Philip K. Dick, Directed by Ridley Scott, Warner Bros., 1982.

Broadcast News. Written & Directed by James L. Brooks, Twentieth Century-Fox, 1987.

Casablanca. Written by Julius Epstein, Philip Epstein, and Howard Koch, Directed by Michael Curtiz, Warner Bros., 1943.

Dazed and Confused. Written & Directed by Richard Linklater, Gramercy Pictures, 1993.

Die Hard. Written by Roderick Thorp, Jeb Stuart, and Steven de Souza, Directed by John McTiernan, Twentieth Century-Fox, 1988.

Fargo. Written & Directed by Joel Coen and Ethan Coen, Polygram Filmed Entertainment, 1996.

The Godfather. Written by Mario Puzo and Francis Ford Coppola, Directed by Francis Ford Coppola, Paramount Pictures, 1972.

Groundhog Day. Written by Danny Rubin and Harold Ramis, Directed by Harold Ramis, Columbia Pictures, 1993.

A League of Their Own. Written by Kim Wilson, Kelly Candaele, and Lowell Ganz, Directed by Penny Marshall, Columbia Pictures, 1992.

National Lampoon's Animal House. Written by Harold Ramis, Douglas Kenney, and Chris Miller, Directed by John Landis, Universal Pictures, 1978.

The Outlaw Josey Wales. Written by Philip Kaufman and Sonia Chernus from the Novel by Forrest Carter, Directed by Clint Eastwood, Warner Bros., 1976.

The Princess Bride. Written by William Goldman, Directed by Rob Reiner, Act III Communications, 1987.

Pulp Fiction. Written by Quentin Tarantino and Roger Avery, Directed by Quentin Tarantino, Miramax, 1994.

Raiders of the Lost Ark. Written by Lawrence Kasdan, George Lucas and Philip Kaufman, Directed by Steven Spielberg, Paramount Pictures, 1981.

Singin' in the Rain. Written by Betty Comden and Adolph Green, Directed by Stanley Donen and Gene Kelly, MGM, 1952.

The Sure Thing. Written by Steve Bloom and Jonathan Roberts, Directed by Rob Reiner, Embassy Pictures, 1985.

Tombstone. Written by Kevin Jarre, Directed by George Cosmatos and Kevin Jarre, Hollywood Pictures, 1993.

The Untouchables. Written by David Mamet and Oscar Fraley, from the Book by Eliot Ness, Directed by Brian DePalma, Paramount Pictures, 1987.

BIBLIOGRAPHY

Cialdini, Robert B. *Influence: The Psychology of Persuasion*. Rev. ed., HarperCollins, 2007.
Crowell, Thomas A. *The Pocket Lawyer for Filmmakers; A Legal Toolkit for Independent Producers*. 3rd ed., Routledge, 2022.
Dancyger, Ken, et al. *Alternative Scriptwriting; Contemporary Storytelling for the Screen*. Routledge, 2023.
Dmytryk, Edward. *On Screen Writing*. Routledge, 2019.
Ellison, Harlan. *Harlan Ellison's Watching*. Underwood-Miller, 1989.
Fink, Edward. *Dramatic Story Structure; A Primer for Screenwriters*. Routledge, 2014.
Goldman, William. *Four Screenplays*. Applause Theatre & Cinema Books, 1995.
Koch, H. *Casablanca: Script and Legend*. The Overlook Press, 1992.
Lasswell, Harold. "The Structure and Function of Communication in Society." *The Communication of Ideas*. Edited by Lyman Bryson, Harper & Row, 1948, pp. 37–51.
Murch, Walter. *In the Blink of an Eye*. 2nd ed., Silman-James Press, 2001.
O'Rourke, P. J., *The Funny Stuff*. Edited by Terry McDonell, Atlantic Monthly Press, 2022.
Rosenblum, Ralph, and Robert Karen. *When the Shooting Stops*. The Viking Press, 1979.
Scholastic Book Services. *Scholastic Dictionary of Synonyms Antonyms Homonyms*. Scholastic Book Services, 1972.
Simmons, Matty. *Fat, Drunk and Stupid; The Inside Story Behind the Making of Animal House*. St. Martins Griffin, 2012.
Stevens, Matt, and Claudia Hunter Johnson. *Script Partners; How to Succeed at Co-Writing for Film & TV*. Routledge, 2016.
Straczynski, J. M. *The Complete Book of Scriptwriting*. Rev. ed., Writers Digest Books, 2002.
Truffaut, Francois. *Hitchcock*. Simon & Schuster Paperbacks, 1984.

INDEX

Note: Page numbers in *italics* indicate a figure on the corresponding page.

action 44, 52, 100–101; bolt 35; brief 55; cheer-able 7; cinematographer with drone in 96; lever 35; onscreen 2; pump 35; reacting to 98; rising action 22–23; in scene description 59, 63, 64; visible 111
advertising 2, 18, 104
ambient sound 114
Antagonist 12–13, 27, 74, 109; at beginning of story 19; Close-Up of *88–89*; default mode 71; Dutch angle/Dutch tilt of 84, *84*; eye level 74, 76–77; at High Angle. 75 77; at Low Angle 74, 76; memorable 13–15; at middle of story 23; Over-the-Shoulder shot 84–85, *85*; rock-throwing 26, 27; in "Universal Horror" style 73
anthropomorphism 12, 14
Applied Screenwriting 14, 62, 72, 117–119, 129, 153; basic screenwriting and 1–9; challenges of 7; defined 6; format for 139; Lasswell's communication model to 6–8, 117; learning to weave story and message and 65
Armorer 35–36, 44

art: and craft of writing script 3–4; image production and 48; martial 45; wall 37
Art Department 32–36
Art Director 32
Assistant Editor 43
Associate Producer 30
audience 1–9, 14–18, 23, 29, 45, 57–58; character's voice heard by 54; final 28; getting attention 34; interest 20; primary 27; setting 21; ultimate 27; *see also* audio; camera; editing; lighting; scene description
audio 2, 57–58, 60–63, 66–67, 77, 105, 120–128, 139–152; ambient/background/natural sound 114; audio-first approach 107; dialogue 108–112; editing 43; elements of 108–115; filter, application of 55; music 112–113; recording 38, *42*; silence 114; sound effects 113–114
Automated Dialogue Replacement (ADR) 40, 111–112

background sound 114
backstory 16, 65–67
bird's-eye view of the scene 94

bits 32; Parenthetical for 55, 111
Blaché, A. G. 3
Bogart, H. 21
Bowie, D. 101
Bowie, Q. 101
Brooker, T. 31

camera 3, 34, 44, 48, 69–70, 113; on-camera talent 44, 90, 110; camerawork 72; distance from subject 78–90; height or level relative to subject 74–78; moving 90–98; setting 39, 78; shooting for the cut 98–99; specialists in 38–39; stabilizer mounts 93, 95
Camera Department 36–40, 71
Camera Operator 36–37, 39, 40
Cast and crew 32, 35–36, 44–45, 50, 53, 63–64, 100, 112, 118
Casting Director 32, 63
characters 6, 23–24, 100, 111; camera distance from 78–90; dialogue 52, 68, 108; essentials of 16–17; introduction of 16; listening 109–110; memory, backstory as 65–67; name 11–12, 52–54; reaction shots 98–99; in scene description 59, 62–65; silence and 114; sound effect 113–114; thoughts and feelings 67; two-shots 86, 99; voice 54–56, 110–111; *see also* Antagonist; Protagonist
Cialdini, R. 14
Cinematographer 30, 32, 36, 40; camera stabilizer mounts 93, 95; with drone in action 94, 96; hand-held movements of 93, 93; Tripod mount 93, 94
cinematography 98, 99, 139
Clapper Loader 37, 38
Close-Up (CU) 33, 82, 84, 88
Communication model 117; audience 7–8; effect 8; medium 7; message 6–7; sender 6
Computer-Generated Imagery (CGI) 39, 43
conciseness 45, 49, 51, 58, 59, 63–64
conflict 18–20, 22–24, 27, 31
consistency 45, 49, 51, 59, 104
continuity editing 101
Coppola, F. F. 3, 30
copyright licenses, permissions of 113

Costume Designer 63
crafts of writing 3–4, 8, 108, 119
Crowell, T. 117
Curtiz, M. 18
Cutaways 98
Cut-Ins 98

Dancyger, K. 117
delivery: line 54; Parenthetical for 55–56, 111
depth of field 90, *91–92*
dialogue 43–44, 58, 64, 98–99; characters 52, 68, 108; as element of audio 108–112; filmography of 153; scene description 68; sound effects 113; Voice-Over and Off-Screen 111; writing 14, 52–54, 68
Dialogue Editor 43
diegetic music 112–113
digital effect 104
digital nonlinear editing (DNLE) 43
Dinehart, S. 8
Directing Department 31–32
Director of Photography (DP) 36, 38–40, 61, 70–71, 75, 77, 118
Directors 3, 31–32, 45, 53–55, 58, 61–62, 77, 100, 118; for camera moves 40; leadership of 70; narrative screenplay 129–139; Producers and 32; two-shot of 86, 99
discontinuity editing 101
Dmytryk, E. 117
dramas 109; series 90; sound-only 3; standard urban 34; story structure 116–117
drones 94; in action 94, 96; final perspective of 96
Dunne, P. 100
Dutch angle/Dutch tilt 84, *84*

editing 98, 100, 108, 117, 139; audio 43; continuity/invisible 101, 103; craft 43; digital nonlinear 43; elements of 102–103, 113; non-continuity/discontinuity 101; Primary Question of 106, 115; rhythm 102–103; rules of 97; software 115; team 37; tempo 102–103; visuals 115
Editor 38–43, 45, 61, 98, 100–104, 118
Editorial Department 40–43

Electrical Department 36, 39–40
electronic media, Parenthetical for 55
Ellison, H. 3
Epstein, J. 18
Epstein, P. 18
eXtreme Close-Up (XCU) 83, 84, 87
eXtreme Long Shot/eXtreme Wide Shot (XLS/XWS) 78, 79

fade-in 103–104, 115
fade-down 115
fade-out 103–104, 115
fade-up 115
feelings of character 67
Fink, E. 116–117
First Assistant Camera 36–37
Foley artist 43, 114
format: Applied Screenwriting 139; novels 48; short story 48; *see also* narrative screenplay; split-column
Full Shot (FS) 78, *80*

Gaffer 40, *41*
German Expressionism 72, 84
Goldilocks Principle 59, 62
Goldman, W. 107
Grip Department 36, 39–40

Hammett, D. 21
hand-held movements 93, *93*
Header, narrative screenplay 49–51, 58, *59*, 64–65, 78
Hitchcock, A. 102
Huston, J. 21, 101

invisible editing 101

J-cut 115
Johnson, C. H. 117

Key Grip 40, *41*
Keyt, J. 117
Koch, H. 18

Laemmle, C. 3
lasercasting 8
Lasswell, H. 6
Lasswell's communication model 6–8, 117
Lawrence, F. 3
L-cut 115

lighting 9, 15, 39, 69; and color 70–72; naturalistic 71; "Universal Lighting" scenario 84
Line Producer 30
Location Manager 32, 62
Long Shot/Wide Shot (LS/WS) 78, 79

Mallett, D. 101
Martin, F. 9
master shot 98
Medium Close-Up (MCU) *81*, 82, 87
Medium Long Shot/Medium Wide Shot (MLS/MWS) *80*, 82
Medium Shot (MS) 33, *81*, 82, 87
Méliès', G. 3
monologue 110–111
montage theory 101
Morahan, A. 101
Motion Pictures Association (MPA) 48
Motion Pictures Association of America (MPAA) 48
Motion Pictures Producers and Distributors of America (MPPDA) 48
moving picture 1, 2, 64, 72, 112
Murch, W. 100, 102
Murphy's Law 96
music 43, 47–48, 72, 108; diegetic and non-diegetic 112–113; as elements of audio 112–113; public domain 113; sound effects 113, 114; video 101
Music Department 43–44

name, characters 11–12, 52–54
narrative screenplay 48, 99, 103, 111, 113–114; dialogue 52–58; example 129–139; header 49–51; scene description 52; shooting for the cut 105
narrowcasting 7
National Lampoon's Animal House 112
naturalistic lighting 71
natural (nat) sound 114
nichecasting 8
non-continuity editing 101
non-diegetic music 112–113
North Star 7, 9, 129
novels 4, 13, 60; format for 48; graphic 21; regular 21; writing 28

Off-Screen: dialogue 111; parentheticals for 54
O'Rourke, P.J. 15
Over-The-Shoulder (OTS) shot 84–85, *85*

Parenthetical 53–54, 108, 110–111; for bits 55, 111; for delivery 55–56; for electronic media 55; for Off-Screen 54; for other languages 54–55; for Voice-Overs 54
Point-of-View (POV) 85
Porter, E. 3
Primary Question 9, 24–27, 58, 99, 118; of audio 115; of editing 106, 115; first 9; other 45–46; of scene descriptions 68; second 27, 117
Producers 29–31, 40, 50–51, 53, 58, 61–62, 70, 100; Directors and 32; Hollywood 56; independent 113, 117; media 36, 45; narrative screenplay 129–139; two-shot of *86*, 99
Producing Department 29–31
Production Designer 29, 32–36, 45, 61–62, 68–69, 100
Production Team 3, 5, 51, 61–63, 70, 104; Art Department 32–36; audio filter, application of 55; Camera Department 36–40; camera moving during shot 94; Cast 44–45; Directing Department 31–32; Editor on 100; Editorial Department 40–43; final product, creating 64; hire to 118; Music Department 43–44; organization of 28; Producing Department 29–31; Sound Department 43–44; using script to make audience 68, 99, 106, 115, 118
professional writing 5, 52
Protagonist 7, 12–13, 32, 54, 65, 97; against Antagonist 26, 75, 109; antiheroic 14; at beginning of story 15–17, 19–21; choker of *83*; Close-Up of *82*, 84; depth of field 90, *91*–92; drone's final perspective of *96*; at end of story 24; eXtreme Close-Up *83*, 84; eXtreme Long Shot/eXtreme Wide Shot of 78, *79*; Full Shot of 78, *80*; Long Shot/Wide Shot 78, *79*; lying underneath tree *26*; Medium Close-Up of *81*, 82; Medium Long Shot/Medium Wide Shot of *80*, 82; Medium Shot of *81*, 82; memorable 13–15; at middle of story 21–22; Over-The-Shoulder shot of 84–85, *85*; sitting in tree *25*; voice-overs 110
public domain music 113
Pulp Fiction (Tarantino) 30

rack focus 90
reaction shots 98–99
Reiner, R. 107
resolution 23–24
rhythm 102–103
Rosenblum, R. 100
rule of thirds 74
Rush, J. 117

scene description 34, 49, 53, 71, 113; action 63, 64; bit 55; characters 59, 62–65; as character's memory 65–67; conciseness 63–64; dialogue 68; in English 52; languages in 54, 111; moving in 64–65; present tense in 52; setting in 59–62; sound effect in 113; story in 65; thoughts and feelings 67
scene heading *see* Header, narrative screenplay
screenwriting: challenge for 14; defined 4; *see also* Applied Screenwriting
script: pulse of 10–26; structure of 47–57; target for 28–45; *see also* story
Second Assistant Camera 36–37
Seger, B. 100
Serling, R. 31
setting 6, 19, 27, 52–53, 100; to audience 21; camera 39, 78; defined 17–18; as part of problem 20; scene 71; in scene description 59–62; stage 69
shooting for the cut, concept of 98–99, 104–106
short story 4, 21, 60; format for 48; writing 59

Shot Framing 58
Shot Number 38, 58
silence 114
slide show with narration approach 110
slugline *see* Header, narrative screenplay
Sound Department 43–44
Sound Designer 43, 45, 55, 68, 108
Sound Editor 43
sound effects (SFX) 113–114
split-column 56–58, 77–78, 90, 93, 99, 111–114; characters 63; example 120–128, 139–152; setting 60; shooting for the cut 105–106; thoughts and feelings 67
split edit 115
Steadicam 93
Steadicam operator 38, 40
Stevens, M. 117
story 55, 98, 104; about individual people 10–12, 44; arts and 4; backstory 16, 65–67; beginning 15–21; care about setting 27; conversation and 68; dramatic structure 116–117; editing 100, 101; end 23–24; entertaining 8; and message, learning to weave 65; middle 21–23; novels (*see* novels); organization of 69; past of 66; people, foundation of 85–86; physical feature/costume piece in 63; primary question 24–27; for Production Designer 34; Protagonist/Antagonist character 12–15; second primary question 27; significance of 3; of sound-only dramas 3 (*see also* dramas); tools 4; video 4; *see also* short story
storytelling 4, 27, 61, 94, 101; camerawork in 72; practical rule of 23; principles 69; reason for motivated camera 97; for screen 117; short film 3; in video 4

story-writing 28
Straczynski, J. M. 21–22

Tarantino, Q. 30
tempo 102–103
thoughts of character 67
Trip to the Moon, A (Méliès') 3
Tripod mount 39–40, 74, 93–94
Truffaut, F. 102
Twain, M. 13
Twilight Zone, The (Serling) 31
two-shots 86, 99

"Universal Horror" lighting effect 71, 73
"Universal Lighting" scenario 84

video 1–3, 29, 57–58, 60–63, 66–67, 77, 90, 105, 111–112, 116–117, 120–128, 139–152; and audio, editing 43; creators 6; cut and 115; demonstration 87; as desired medium 7; documentaries and corporate 101–102; entertainment 56; in fade-in 103; fiction 54; first 74; games 8; independent and inexpensive work 90; micro-budget 109; modern 43; music 101; needlepoint 87; online 15, 23; own personal stamp on 6; paying for 6; promo 109; realm 12; short-form 14, 107–109; smartphone 36; social media 9; storytelling 4; streamers, advent of 8; time and 97; time code 38; tools of 5, 8; training 110; videography 75; viral 118–119; write scripts for 4
Voice-Over 67–68, 101, 113; dialogue 110–111; parentheticals for 54

wasted page space 61
Weapons Master *see* Armorer

zoom 87–88

Printed in the USA
CPSIA information can be obtained
at www.ICGtesting.com
LVHW021736041124
795688LV00040B/1264